Ballet
as
Body
Language

Joan McConnell

Ballet as Body Language

With the Special Collaboration of

Teena McConnell

HARPER & ROW, PUBLISHERS

NEW YORK, HAGERSTOWN, SAN FRANCISCO, LONDON

To

B and Richard, who made it
all possible

Photo credits: Michael Avedon: pages xvi, 9 (right), 122; Fred Fehl: page 85; Milly Matacia: pages 99, 103, 105, 107, 109, 125; Van Picture Service: page 101. All other photos courtesy Foto Bazzechi

Designed by Stephanie Krasnow

Library of Congress Cataloging in Publication Data

McConnell, Joan.
  Ballet as body language.

  Includes index.
  1. Ballet.   I. McConnell, Teena, joint author.
II. Title.
GV1787.M25   1977   792.8   77-3760
ISBN 0-06-012957-3
ISBN 0-06-012964-6 pbk.
_____

 78 79 80 81 10 9 8 7 6 5 4 3 2

Acknowledgments

Both Teena and I would like to thank all the people who, directly or indirectly, have inspired us to write this book.

A special word of appreciation to our outstanding teachers: to George Balanchine, who made us love ballet; to Felia Doubrovska, who taught us the elegant bearing of the Maryinsky School; to Muriel Stuart, who imparted to us the precious training she acquired under Anna Pavlova; to Albertine Maxwell, who opened our eyes to the richness of dance forms other than ballet; to Edna Dieman and Julia Bennett, who taught us the importance of tradition in every kind of dance; to Alexandra Danilova, who shared her consummate artistry.

Our sincere thanks to Giancarlo Cioni, who has kept us "warm" during those long, cold winters, to Paola at Mantellassi's, who has kept us stepping, to Jole Carletti, who creates wonders with her magic fingers, and to Toodie.

And finally our deepest thanks to all the readers and listeners but especially to Pearl, whose patience and thoughtful suggestions have improved the book.

Contents

Foreword

I first saw Teena McConnell as a ballet dancer in Balanchine's *Don Quixote,* in which she was one of four ladies in waiting. I had met her a year before at a voting booth, but was now seated too far from the stage to identify her in her elaborate court costume. Her sister Joan, then my graduate student at Columbia, who had invited us to the performance at Lincoln Center, challenged me to pick her out. I couldn't. But I was struck by the grace and verve of one of the four ladies in the line, and remarked as much. Joan smiled. "That's Teena!" she said.

This was my first attendance at a full-fledged ballet, a form of art in which I had only a perfunctory interest. Since then, thanks largely to the McConnell sisters, I have become an enthusiast. Teena's grace is that of a gazelle. The New York City Ballet, of which she has been a member since the age of sixteen, is in her heart, blood, brain and supple muscles. It is her life and her breath. And she knows how to fire others with her enthusiasm. "It is dynamic, creative to the full!" she says. "It is the expression of life in action!" And she makes it live.

In the New York City Ballet, as in New Jersey's Garden State Ballet (Teena is New Jersey born, bred and educated), her specialty is Tchaikovsky's *The Nutcracker,* in which she dances various solo parts. The Sugar Plum Fairy is her customary role when she performs for the Garden State. But her favorite role is the pas de deux in *Agon.*

As a member of the Balanchine ensemble, she has danced in every part of the United States, in Canada, in Israel, in Europe on both sides of the Iron Curtain—which does not exist so far as the arts are concerned. The touring troupe's greatest international triumphs were in the Soviet Union, where cheering audiences threw flowers and candy on the stage. England, Italy,

Greece, Germany, Austria, Poland, Yugoslavia are among the countries that acclaimed Balanchine's performers. Only in France, at a difficult moment in international relations between de Gaulle and the United States, was the reception less than enthusiastic.

In addition to her regular organizational performances, Teena has developed a unique offering in collaboration with her older sister, who was herself a ballet dancer before she turned into a linguistic scholar and professor of Italian at Stanford University's Italian Center in Florence. Joan is a superb lecturer, in both English and Italian. As she describes the intricacies of ballet steps to rapt audiences at women's clubs and similar organizations, here and abroad, Teena illustrates the movements and postures with her own brand of effortless grace. The result is spectacular. So impressed were certain viewers in Brazil, that the sisters have been invited to organize a ballet school there.

Teena McConnell was among the original student volunteers who joined Fred and Evelyn Danieli in 1953 when they formed the company that was to be the kernel of the Garden State Ballet, officially launched in 1960. Between 1956 and 1959 the student group gave frequent demonstrations at the Paper Mill Playhouse in Millburn. Before that time there had been no organized ballet company in New Jersey, though New York–based companies toured frequently. As far back as 1939, Ballet Caravan, a forerunner of the New York City Ballet, had given occasional performances at the Paper Mill Playhouse. In the 1940s and early 1950s, Newark's Symphony Hall had at times been graced by performances offered by the Ballet Russe de Monte Carlo. The Garden State ensemble has performed exclusively in New Jersey.

There has always been an unofficial form of collaboration between the big Balanchine organization and the more modest Garden State Ballet. Fred Danieli prefers Balanchine's ballets to all others, and presents some of them, with Balanchine's approval. Further, Danieli has supplied the New York City Ballet with much budding talent. No fewer than six of Balanchine's present company are Danieli-trained.

Teena McConnell has traveled all over the world, generally with her sister. She is familiar with most African countries, with the Middle and Far East, with Latin America. Her plans for the future are firmly based on a continuance of her present activities. She regards her profession not merely as a career, but as a mission of good will. Her visits to foreign lands, particularly in the Communist world, have convinced her that the message of the performing arts is international; that here, if anywhere, lies the true spirit of *détente*, shorn of selfish national and economic interests. The cult of pure beauty knows no boundaries, no limitations of language, race, color, nationality, religion or political belief. The performing arts in general, and her beloved ballet in particular, are on a plane where all human beings, without exception, can meet in perfect equality and friendship.

*   *   *

From my own professional point of view as a linguist (but thanks largely to my observation of the McConnell sisters), I have come to view the ballet as something far closer to my specialty than I had at first envisaged.

Language may be viewed, narrowly and etymologically, as that which is produced by the tongue. But there is a much broader interpretation of what constitutes language: that which serves the purposes of both communication and self-expression. In this wider sense, language goes far beyond the spoken and written word. It includes such things as visible, audible, perceptible symbols (like traffic lights and factory whistles) that convey a message and a meaning, or that express the thoughts, feelings, sentiments, moods of a single person, even in the absence of an audience.

Gestural language has a long and brilliant history that probably antedates that of speech, and is illustrated in such elaborate forms as the hand gestures by which American Indian tribes of different speech communicated with one another, and the various systems ingeniously worked out for the use of deaf-mutes. The role of spontaneous, unconscious gestures, bodily postures and movements, changes of facial expression, has given rise to a science of "body language," a branch of kinetics, now skillfully and effectively applied in the field of intercultural relations, as well as within a single culture.

It is to this division of linguistic science that the art of dancing makes its bid for admission. The ballet is not merely a form of language, but the most exalted, most "classical" branch of the language of the dance, comparable to the spoken and written tongue of poetry. Like the classical poetic tongue, it has balance and style, rhythm and rhyme, aesthetic grace and symbolic meaning. Its skilled practitioner must be not merely supple and elastic but highly imaginative and prompt to interpret the moods and recondite messages of the ballet's creators and choreographers, as well as of the original literary authors and musical composers. On the stage, the ballet dancer is the conveyor to the audience of the thoughts and sentiments of Shakespeare and Cervantes, of Tchaikovsky, Stravinsky and Bernstein, as well as of Petipa, Balanchine and Robbins. The ballet weaves into a single pattern story and music, legend, myth and reality. It is the quintessence of poetry in motion.

MARIO PEI

Preface

When I decided to give up professional ballet and go to college, one of my ballet teachers nodded knowingly as I explained that it was impossible for me to combine a dance career with college. I was confident that she not only understood but even supported my choice. Maybe she did, but I was slightly taken by surprise when she answered, "Yes, yes. You vant school, you no vant dance. But you, dear, no forget dance—never, n-e-v-e-r!" Maybe her thick Russian accent added a touch of special significance to that ominous-sounding "never." Maybe I was projecting my own mixed feelings about a decision which she had nonetheless accepted as final. Despite the real or imagined ambiguity I read into her answer, I dared not ask for an explanation—which ballet teachers in my day never gave their students. And so, five minutes later, I walked out of the School of American Ballet for the last time.

I then went to Sarah Lawrence College, where my faculty adviser marveled at my refusal to continue dance. I had given up ballet in order to go to college, and therefore I would take only "serious," academically oriented courses. Today this reasoning seems silly, and yet fifteen years ago, dance was not generally considered on the same level with the so-called heavy courses. Soon I became involved in serious linguistic studies, which finally drew me into academia and a college teaching career.

It took me several years to realize that my old teacher at the School of American Ballet had been right. I had given up dancing as a career, but I could not forget dance. Ballet was in my blood, in my body, even though the muscles had lost their flexibility. I would instinctively start to dance as soon as I heard the familiar refrains of ballet music. And I heard them often after my sister Teena joined the New York City Ballet Company.

Life plays strange tricks on all of us. I, who had so adamantly rejected ballet after my decision to go to college, found myself thrust back into the ballet world, though this time not on the professional level. I went to the ballet to see my sister and act as her "personal" critic. I went often, sometimes alone, sometimes with my mother and sometimes with friends. Since some of these friends had never seen a ballet, I gave them quick explanations. Their enthusiasm grew as they began to familiarize themselves with the basic principles of ballet. They started to know what to look for and how to appreciate good ballet. I felt particularly challenged by the "tough," masculine stereotyped reaction that ballet was fine for sissies. I may not have converted all my friends, but at least those "superman" types had to admit that ballet was hard, athletic work.

It is difficult to remember exactly how Teena and I decided to prepare a joint lecture demonstration on ballet appreciation. We set up a program geared for an audience that knew nothing about ballet. I did the lecture portion, while Teena did the actual dance demonstration. We illustrated the basic steps that govern ballet, and explained their importance. In other words, we wanted the audience to understand what they were looking at. We used the daily class as the starting point. Then we showed how the basic movements are first studied separately, then combined into progressively more difficult patterns till they are worthy of performance levels. At the end of this explanation, Teena performed excerpts from one or more ballets to show the audience the "final" product.

Naturally, our early demonstrations were short and simple, but they interested our audiences. Slowly we expanded our lecture demonstrations into a two-hour show with music and a male partner for Teena. We prepared several versions—one for schools, another for adult audiences, and even one for performances abroad.

The best part of these demonstrations for both of us was reaching our audiences. We tried to maintain an informal atmosphere and encourage questions from the audience because the demonstration was really their show. For me, the most fulfilling moment happened when Teena started to perform. As soon as she stepped onto the stage in full make-up and costume, the audience invariably felt the magic of the performance. I never watched Teena, but looked instead at the spectators' reactions to ballet. These were certainly not the reactions of experts or dance critics; they were merely the reactions of people who were beginning to have an idea of what ballet was. Ballet was no longer a series of strange, incomprehensible movements that had no relation to their lives. Instead the audience realized that ballet was total body language —not the only form of body language, not necessarily what they considered the most beautiful or the most convincing or the most anything. But it was a form of communication, and as such commanded respect.

Only recently some friends suggested that Teena and I convert our lecture demonstrations into a book. Our initial reaction was negative since a book, we felt, would lose many of the effects of the stage. But their confidence finally convinced us. The presentation follows the general lines of our lecture demonstrations, but we have expanded certain topics and introduced new ones. We have tried to add a touch of "visual" clarity through the use of photographs. Despite the inevitable differences between a book and a live performance, we have attempted to keep the same informal spirit of the demonstrations, and hope to arouse the same enthusiastic response in our readers. And maybe some of the readers will also understand why my old ballet teacher said that it is impossible to forget ballet.

Chapter 1

The Background of Ballet

If you asked ten people to tell you what ballet is, you would probably get ten different answers. One would describe a ballerina in a white tutu. Another would say that ballet is *Swan Lake,* while still another would insist that all ballerinas are Russian. And you might even have an intellectual who defined ballet as stylized dance. Undoubtedly there is a portion of truth in all these definitions. Ballerinas wear white tutus, but they also wear blue ones, and red ones and long ones—or perhaps plain black leotards. Certainly *Swan Lake* is the epitome of classical ballet, but not all ballets were, are, or even aim to be classical. Russia has produced a dazzling array of great ballerinas, but then again, so have Italy, France, England, Denmark and the United States. Ballet is stylized dance, but stylized dance is not always ballet. Thus while all these definitions pinpoint certain significant aspects of ballet, they overlook its general characteristics.

To understand what ballet is, perhaps one should first think about what dance is. Dance is a series of connected, meaningful movements which externalize inner feelings. It is ephemeral, and until the recent development of film and video tapes, it left no lasting record. This lack of permanency is the very quality that makes dance unique. Even though the same dance may be repeated by the same dancer, it is always different. Unlike painting and sculpture, dance cannot be displayed in a museum corner.

Dance formed an important part of primitive cultures, and established a type of social unity among the members of a particular community. On the basis of anthropological studies, it seems that dance originated as an attempt

Ballet is body language

by primitive man to imitate birds, animals and, more generally, the mysterious forces of nature. In this way, he probably hoped to create a magical link between himself and the external forces beyond his control and his understanding.

As man's life styles changed and progressed, so did his dances. In many civilizations, dance lost its original magical or religious functions and became a form of popular entertainment or recreational pastime. In many countries, it still serves an important role in the ritual of courtship. It has often been used as a means of improving or strengthening the body. Today in our Western culture, where some forms of dance are considered art, dedicated professionals spend long years training arduously to master its techniques. These dancers no longer form an integral part of the community, since their function is primarily peripheral.

If we want to discover the origins of ballet, we have to go back to the Italian Renaissance. After a series of devastating experiences including the Black Plague, a surge of new political, commercial and artistic activity swept through Italy, and later the rest of Europe. Fresh ideas poured into Italy, broadening man's horizons, especially in the arts. The merchants, bankers and princes were exposed to these different stimuli, and developed a new sense of beauty that reflected the influence of the classical civilizations of Greece and Rome. The Renaissance man rejected the medieval emphasis on otherworldliness, and found instead new enthusiasm in studying man and his potential— especially his artistic potential—in this world.[1]

The word "ballet" comes from the Italian verb *ballare,* meaning "to dance," and its derivative *ballo* ("a dance") and the diminutive *balletto* (literally, "little dance"). Though *balli* and *balletti* were originally types of dances, in the fifteenth and sixteenth centuries the words referred to court spectacles, which combined dance, music, song and poetry. The dancing itself was formal and stylized, and based on the court dances of the period (the sarabande, the galliard, the pavane, the courante). These court fetes were performed in the great halls of the princely Renaissance palaces. The nobles and honored guests watched from three sides, while the less noble spectators sat in the balconies. Because of the three-sided perspective, the intricate floor patterns performed by all the dancers were more important than any individual dancers.

While the roots of ballet are Italian, the first "real" ballet, *Le Ballet*

Comique de la Reine, was performed at the French court in 1581, to celebrate the marriage of Mlle de Vaudemont, the queen's sister, to the Duke of Joyeuse. The choreographer, Balthasar de Beaujoyeaux, was an Italian musician (his name was originally Baldassarino di Belgiojoso) who had captured the favor of the queen mother, Catherine de' Medici, at the Paris court. For this lavish spectacle, Balthasar combined dance and comedy into a harmonious unity so that, in his own words, the dance would speak, and the comedy would sing and dance. His highly successful production bored none of the guests despite its length—the performance started at 10 P.M. and ended at 3:30 A.M.

The French monarchs continued to patronize these court ballets, though in less elaborate versions because the cost of financing spectacles like Balthasar's had become exorbitant. During the reign of Henry IV (1589–1610), eighty court ballets were performed. It is important to remember that most of the dancing during this period was performed by the noblemen—the ladies were not permitted to participate—who wore elaborate masks, sometimes made of gold mesh. Dancing was considered an essential part of every nobleman's training since it improved his carriage, his grace and his ability in combat. After the introduction of firearms, brute strength in battle had become obsolete, at least for the nobility.

During the reign of Louis XIV (1643–1715), ballet ceased to be performed solely by amateurs. The king himself was an excellent dancer, and took daily lessons from Pierre Beauchamps, one of the most famous dancers and choreographers of the day. The inspiration for Louis's epithet "the Sun King" (*Le Roi Soleil*) dates back to 1653, when he danced the part of the Sun in *Le Ballet de la Nuit.* He danced in all the court spectacles until his obesity forced him to retire in 1670.

In 1661, Louis founded the Royal Academy of Dance, and a few years later, the Royal Academy of Music.[2] This was the first time that ballet had received royal recognition. The school of dance attached to the Paris Opera (founded in 1669) was, however, far more influential both in the development of ballet as a separate art form and in the formation of great dancers. As its first ballet master, Beauchamps formulated some basic ballet principles, including the five positions. He also pioneered a kind of dance shorthand.

Jean Baptiste Lully (Lulli in Italian; 1632–1687) was a Florentine composer and dancer who became director of the Paris Opera. Along with

Molière and Beauchamps, he choreographed many important ballets. In 1691, Mlle Lafontaine made ballet history when she appeared in *Le Triomphe de l'Amour,* thus becoming the first professional female dancer.

In addition to the new professional status of ballet, another important change took place. At this time most of the court ballets were performed in the French royal theater, which had been built by Richelieu according to Italian specifications, with the stage raised and slightly sloped.

This innovation produced two important changes in the ballets of the day. First of all, it created an atmosphere of greater professionalism, since the distance between the audience and the performers was increased. Secondly—but undoubtedly more important—the raised stage changed the spectators' perspective, because they viewed only from the front. For the spectacles in the palace halls, the dances had been based primarily on intricate floor patterns which could be seen from three sides. When the dancers performed on the new, elevated stage, however, the choreography and dance movements had to be adjusted. Because of the one-sided perspective, the effect of intricate floor patterns by groups of dancers was lost; therefore, the movements of the individual dancer became more interesting to the audience. This innovation also forced the dancer to move from side to side so that the audience could see what he was doing. In order to move gracefully, the dancer had to develop the so-called turnout—that is, the position whereby the dancer's feet turned to the sides rather than to the front. The emphasis on turnout also made it easier for the dancer to execute brilliant leaps and turns.

Generally speaking, the eighteenth century was the era of the great male dancers. The most important dancing dynasty was the Vestris family. The father, Gaetano (1729–1808), was a passionate Florentine who had studied at the Paris Opera under the famous Louis Dupré. Vestris was intensely popular in his serious, heroic roles, and thanks to the help of his brother, gained the coveted title *Le Dieu de la Danse* ("the God of the Dance"). His son Auguste—born from an illicit relationship with the well-known dancer Mlle Allard—achieved even greater fame. Though very short, Auguste had remarkable elevation and impeccable technique. He performed for the last time at the age of seventy-five, when he partnered Marie Taglioni, who was then thirty-one! Auguste's pride, however, matched his brilliant dancing. He publicly announced that he, Voltaire and the king of Prussia were the three greatest men in Europe.

Though male dancers dominated the ballet world, women were beginning to make headway. At this time, the female dancers were hampered by their long, heavy costumes and imposing wigs. Marie Camargo (1710–1770) caused a scandal when she shortened her skirt, and danced in slippers with no heels in order to show off her gay, light steps and her excellent jumps. Her rival Marie Sallé (1707–1756) went one step farther when, in 1734, she shed her heavy skirt and corset, and wore a simple muslin tunic in her own ballet *Pygmalion*. Sallé thus became the first woman choreographer. Anne Heinel (1753–1808), who married Gaetano Vestris in 1792, was a German ballerina and supposedly the first woman to perform a double pirouette. Madeleine Guimard (1743–1816) was perhaps the greatest dancer of the day, despite her unfashionably skinny body and her pockmarked face.

The great ballet reformer of the eighteenth century was Jean Georges Noverre (1727–1810), who made his debut with the Paris Opera at the age of sixteen and became its ballet master at twenty. He believed that ballet in France had been unable to become an independent art form because of certain basic handicaps—old-fashioned costumes and wigs, which encumbered the dancers; masks, which hid the dancers' expressions; emphasis on sheer technical virtuosity; poor choreography, which strung together unconnected dances. To revitalize ballet, technical skill had to be combined with dramatic expressiveness.

In his famous *Letters on Dancing and Ballet,* published in Stuttgart in 1760, Noverre maintained that ballet movements should be brilliant and dramatically expressive, that the plots must be simplified and unified through the omission of extraneous material, that there should be a harmonious relationship among the dancing, music, plot and scenery, and that the traditional formal gestures in the pantomime had to be modernized. Ballet should never be mere entertainment; it should be, in Noverre's words, *ballet d'action*— ballet with plot and action. Without these two elements, ballet would never develop into an independent art form. Like Fokine one hundred fifty years later, Noverre believed that ballet was a happy marriage between technique and feeling, blessed with genius.

Noverre's reforms were too radical for the traditional French court. He staged his great ballets at the court of Württemberg (1760), in Vienna (1767–74) and at the King's Theater in London (1782, 1788–89). Though unsuccessful in realizing all his reforms and in establishing ballet as an independent art, he was one of the most influential figures in the history of ballet.

While the French dancers and choreographers resisted the novelty of Noverre's ideas, ballet was flourishing in Italy. The Neapolitan Salvatore Viganò (1769–1821), a pupil of the famous French dancer and choreographer Dauberval, tried to carry out Noverre's theories at the Academy of Dance at La Scala in Milan. In particular, he helped streamline the pantomime gestures, which were necessary for the plot.

Probably the most important Italian dancer/choreographer of the time was Carlo Blasis (1795–1878), a Neapolitan noble with the reputation of being a universal genius. He was chief dancer at La Scala, dancer and choreographer at the King's Theater in London, and perhaps most important of all, a great teacher at the Academy of Dance in Milan. There he trained some of the most brilliant Italian dancers, who later took the Italian style to the Maryinsky Theater in St. Petersburg. Blasis was an avid student of sculpture and anatomy.

At seventeen, he published his first important book, *A Theoretical, Practical and Elementary Treatise on the Art of Dancing*. In his famous *Code of Terpsichore* (1830), he codified ballet technique and discussed the problem of equilibrium and balance. He developed geometric patterns governing body movement. He is credited with the invention of a new position, the so-called attitude, whereby the dancer stands on one leg and extends the other behind

The attitude

him in the air, bending it at the knee. Blasis supposedly derived this famous position from Giambologna's statue of Mercury.

During his years as director of the Academy of Dance at La Scala, Blasis established a series of rules for the students. Before being admitted to the academy, the pupils had to pass a medical test to make sure they were in good health and had no hereditary diseases. They could be no younger than eight and no older than twelve (fourteen for the boys). The students were bound for eight years, and were apprentices during the first three. After graduation they were guaranteed financial security for the rest of their lives. Interestingly enough, these basic guidelines were adopted in most European dance academies, and are still followed in the state dance schools of the U.S.S.R.

In the first half of the nineteenth century—the Age of Romanticism—revolt against the hallowed symbols of classicism extended far beyond the arts and literature. It became a life style for daring intellectuals and a source of inspiration for political activists, particularly in Italy. Romanticism revolutionized nineteenth-century ballet. The ballerina was glorified, and the male dancer, except in Russia and Denmark, was relegated to a position of secondary importance. In some cases, the aversion toward the male dancer was so strong that his part was danced by a woman disguised as a man—the so-called *danseuse en travesti*. Much of the prejudice against male dancers can be traced back to these Romantic reforms.

Woman became an enchanted, unattainable dream that man could never capture. She floated away—quite literally in many Romantic ballets, which had enchanted fairies flying through the air by means of complicated wires. Toe dancing was introduced because it corresponded to the artistic criteria of the day. The ballerinas wore long white tulle dresses which accentuated the dreamy, ethereal qualities of their movements. These shimmering, unearthly ballets came to be known as *ballets blancs,* or "white ballets."

The original Romantic ballet is *La Sylphide,* which Filippo Taglioni choreographed for his famous daughter, Marie, in 1832. Marie Taglioni (1804–1884), often called the first Christian dancer because of her light, airy, otherworldly style, epitomized the ideals of the Romantic ballerina. She was the rage of Paris. Chic Parisian women wore their hair *à la Sylphide*—parted in the center like Taglioni's in the ballet. Taglioni is also credited with the introduction of toe dancing, though less famous dancers had stood on pointe before her. The only support in Taglioni's slippers came from the heavy darning under the toes; therefore the steps she performed on toe were limited to graceful poses and a few arabesques.

Taglioni, though one of the greatest ballerinas of all time, faced stiff competition from the Viennese-born Fanny Elssler (1810–1884), who, in the opinion of the critics, represented the pagan, earthy side of Romanticism. In contrast to Taglioni, who was unattractive and round-shouldered, Elssler captivated her public with her great beauty and passionate dancing. While Taglioni was famed for her elevation, Elssler was essentially a terre à terre dancer—that is, her feet left the ground only so she could point her toes. She also introduced national dances into the ballet. Elssler danced all over Europe, and from 1840 to 1842 made a triumphal tour of the United States, where her partner was the American dancer George Washington Smith. During her trip to the New World, she supposedly kicked a sailor who had the unfortunate idea of trying to rob her. Her kick was so violent that the poor man died a few days later!

Fanny Cerrito (1817–1909)—the "divine" Fanny, as she was called—was another great Italian ballerina, second only to Taglioni in international fame. She was renowned for her voluptuous figure and her vivacious dancing. The beautiful Danish ballerina Lucile Grahn (1819–1907), a pupil of the Danish teacher August Bournonville,[3] joined the ranks of the great Italian ballerinas. She danced with Cerrito and Taglioni in the *Pas de Trois*.

The two faces of Romanticism, Christian and pagan, were embodied in the Italian ballerina Carlotta Grisi (1819–1899). She was a source of inspiration to Théophile Gautier, the French author and critic, who wrote the libretto for *Giselle*. Jean Coralli was credited with the choreography, though Jules Perrot, Grisi's husband, really created most of the dances; Adolphe Adam wrote the score. In the first act of the ballet, Grisi represented the physical, while in the haunting second act, she became the spiritual. *Giselle* is one of the few Romantic ballets that have come down to us, and along with the classical *Swan Lake,* it is the supreme test of a ballerina's technical virtuosity and her dramatic ability.

One of the glorious moments during the "golden age of ballet" (1830–45) was the performance of the *Pas de Quatre* (choreography by Perrot) that Taglioni, Grisi, Cerrito and Grahn danced in London in 1845. The ballet, an immediate success, was danced only five times by the original cast, though it has since been revived by several ballet companies.

The Romantic ballerina

The Classical ballerina

After 1850, French ballet began to deteriorate because there had been too much emphasis placed on the star and too little on the other dancers and on the choreography. Ballet was flourishing in Russia, however, thanks to the patronage of the czars. Western-style dancing, imported into Russia by Peter the Great as part of his general project to westernize his country, caught on very quickly. The nobles in their large, isolated estates trained some of the serfs for performances in their private theaters. Thus, uniquely, the love of dance became deeply rooted among the Russian people, not only among the nobles.

Charles Louis Didelot (1767–1836), a pupil of Dauberval, Noverre and Auguste Vestris, brought the French-style ballet to St. Petersburg in 1816. He choreographed many ballets, and improved the teaching methods in the imperial schools. Louis Duport (1781–1853), one of Auguste Vestris's rivals, left the Paris Opera, and caused a sensation in Russia when he performed Didelot's ballets. The Dane Christian Johansson (1817–1903), a pupil of Bournonville, became a leading dancer in Russia, and even partnered Taglioni on her last tour, in 1842. His teaching methods were also influential in improving ballet standards in Russia.

Russian ballet reached its height under the guidance of the French-born Marius Petipa (1819–1910). In 1847, he arrived in St. Petersburg as premier danseur, and in 1862, succeeded Jules Perrot as ballet master. In this position, Petipa revolutionized ballet in Russia, and created what is known as the classical style. He choreographed more than fifty new ballets (*The Sleeping Beauty, The Nutcracker, Raymonda, Don Quichotte, La Bayadère*), revised seventeen old works (including *Swan Lake*) and prepared the dance sequences for thirty-five operas. The choreography in all his ballets followed a fixed order. In his lavish five-to-six-act ballets, there was a definite division between pantomime and dancing. The "real" dancing was always separate from the story, and included solo or demi-solo variations, character dances, and the inevitable pas de deux, with its romantic adagio, separate variations for the ballerina and her partner, and the final coda. The plot and pantomime merely served as a background for the ballerina's virtuosity. Petipa had important composers like Tchaikovsky and Glazunov write ballet scores according to his rigid specifications.

Petipa was a brilliant teacher, and perfected the Russian technique, which has been universally acclaimed ever since. When Petipa arrived in Russia the great dancers were all foreign, but when he died, in 1910, they were all Russian.

Russian ballet can best be described as a skillful combination of the French and the Italian ballet styles flavored with a dash of Russian genius. In the late nineteenth century, most of the outstanding dancers—Virginia Zucchi and Pierina Legnani in particular—were Italians, trained at the Academy of Dance at La Scala, which was famous for its brilliant technique. The great Enrico Cecchetti (1850–1928), born into a dancing family, brought the Milanese teaching method to St. Petersburg, where he trained some of the most famous Russian dancers: Pavlova, Nijinsky, Preobrajenska, Karsavina, Kschessinska and Fokine. His rigid system of teaching was later codified by Idzikowski and Beaumont. The Cecchetti method still influences English and Italian ballet.

Like all good things, Petipa's choreographic formula lost much of its luster through overuse. Many of the younger dancers and aspiring choreographers, especially Michel Fokine (1880–1942), rebelled against the great master's rules, and criticized his conventional approach to ballet. Since Fokine's ideas were too revolutionary for the staid Russian audiences, he left St. Petersburg and joined Diaghilev in Paris in 1909.

Though Fokine was a great dancer in his own right, he will be remembered first as a choreographer (*Les Sylphides,* in which he evoked Taglioni's Romantic era, *Carnaval, Scheherazade, Petrouchka*) and then as a dance reformer. Following in the footsteps of Noverre and Blasis, he felt that ballet should combine technical virtuosity with dramatic expressiveness. He despised Petipa's use of the plot as a foil for the prima ballerina's technique. He abhorred the stereotyped costumes, which never really changed, despite a change in plot and setting. The imperial ballerinas wore the inevitable tutu, with an added rose or ribbon for ethnic flavor. Pointe work was used to create spectacular effects, even though these movements often contradicted the body's natural harmony. Fokine revolted against the star system, and advocated a more democratic approach through greater use of the corps de ballet. He restored the male dancer to a position of importance after decades of female domination.

In his letter of June 6, 1914, to the London *Times,* Fokine explained his famous five principles: The choreography of a ballet should reflect the subject matter accurately and maintain ethnic authenticity. Dancing and pantomime have no meaning unless they are integrated into the dramatic action. Conventional pantomime gestures should be eliminated, and replaced by significant movements of the entire body: "man can be and should be expressive from head to foot." Group dances by the corps de ballet must be an integral part of the dramatic action, not merely ornamental additions. There should be complete equality among the choreographer, the dancer and the musician since ballet is a harmonious unity of the efforts of all three.

The twentieth century marked a series of important changes in ballet. First of all, the center of ballet switched from Russia back to France, mainly because of Serge Diaghilev's (1872–1929) dissatisfaction with the stuffy conventionalism of Russian ballet. His opening night production in Paris on May 18, 1909, included a series of short, one-act ballets starring great artists like Anna Pavlova, Tamara Karsavina, Bronislava Nijinska, her brother Vaslav Nijinsky, and Michel Fokine. This performance was an immediate success, and stimulated new interest in an art that had fallen into disfavor in Western Europe.

The second major change was Diaghilev's and Fokine's revolt against the Russian *danse d'école*—that is, the classical ballet style. The effects of this break with tradition were positive inasmuch as they enabled dynamic choreographers like Fokine and Nijinsky to experiment with new expressive mediums. Nijinsky's *Afternoon of a Faun* caused a sensation in Paris, and his *Rite of Spring* to Stravinsky's music so enraged the audience that many walked out! But the revolt had negative repercussions, since it represented a break with the past. This lack of continuity created a sense of confusion, especially after the great Russian dancers trained in the imperial schools had died.

Finally the success of the ballet was placed in the hands of a new figure, the impresario, who was more often than not an outsider to the ballet world. Though highly intelligent and well versed in the arts, Diaghilev was not a dancer, but only a lover of the dance. Diaghilev was the first commoner to control an art that had formerly been reserved for the nobles. Thus the break with tradition also implied a democratization of an art form that had sprung from the courts of European nobility.

The Diaghilev Company danced all over Europe, and exposed the audiences to some of the greatest dancers of all times. Vaslav Nijinsky (1890–1950) was famed for his amazing elevation and exotic movements. His performances in two of Fokine's most famous ballets, *Les Sylphides* and *Le Spectre de la Rose,* won him international acclaim, which vied perhaps only with Taglioni's. Unfortunately his dancing career ended abruptly when he went insane. Before his illness, Nijinsky partnered the most famous ballerinas of his day—Tamara Karsavina, who fled Russia in 1917, as well as the immortal Pavlova.

Anna Pavlova (1885–1931) danced for Diaghilev after she left Russia, but her association with the company was short-lived because she disagreed with the impresario's ideas on ballet, especially his preference for male dancers. After establishing her home in England, she formed her own company, composed mostly of English girls, and toured. Despite the troupe's mediocre dancing and limited repertoire, Pavlova charmed her audiences with her graceful, seemingly effortless style. She added her own personal touch of genius to every role she danced. More than any other single dancer, she was responsible for stimulating the average person's interest in ballet.

Diaghilev's death in 1929 threw the ballet world into turmoil. At first it seemed as if his troupe would not survive, but in 1932, after a series of tumultuous vicissitudes, Colonel W. de Basil formed a new company, Les Ballets Russes de Monte Carlo, thus restoring a shaky equilibrium. Despite the initial confusion, Diaghilev's death brought about positive long-range results since it encouraged the formation of various new ballet companies in

Europe and in the U.S. By the 1930s it had become quite clear that a ballet empire under the control of one man had become obsolete. By breaking the continuity of the ballet tradition, Diaghilev had stimulated, albeit indirectly, the growth of national ballet companies. Thus geographical diversification would become an increasingly important factor in ballet.

After 1929, part of Diaghilev's company settled in England. Marie Rambert (born Miriam Rambach) and Ninette de Valois (born Edris Stannus) were particularly influential in creating the company that, after a series of complicated transformations, became the Royal Ballet. In 1956, Queen Elizabeth II incorporated, by royal charter, the Sadler's Wells Ballet, the Sadler's Wells Theater Ballet and the Sadler's Wells School under the general title Royal Ballet. Alicia Markova (Alice Marks), one of the outstanding English ballerinas, danced as guest artist with this company. Her partnership with Anton Dolin (Patrick Healey-Kay) made ballet history. The greatest ballerina of the British company was undoubtedly Dame Margot Fonteyn (Margaret Hookham), who maintained a position of unchallenged supremacy in the ballet hierarchy.

The characteristic French style was "Russianized" when Serge Lifar, one of Diaghilev's greatest male dancers, joined the Paris Opera in 1929. As ballet master, Lifar was a creative, though controversial, figure. He succeeded in revitalizing French ballet so that it regained much of its former prestige. The other major figure in French ballet is Roland Petit, who left the Paris Opera to form his own company, Les Ballets de Paris.

The great Russian dancers Kschessinska and Trefilova, who left Russia in 1917, and Preobrajenska, who left in 1922, settled in Paris and opened ballet schools. Many of their pupils joined de Basil's Ballets Russes. This company was famous for the "baby ballerinas"—Irina Baronova, Tamara Toumanova, Tatiana Riabouchinska—as well as for Alexandra Danilova, who had left Russia in 1924 with George Balanchine. Balanchine was de Basil's first ballet master, but left shortly afterward because of personal friction with the management. He was succeeded by Leonide Massine, who had also been a dancer and choreographer in Diaghilev's company. In 1938, the Ballets Russes split in two, under Massine and de Basil—but neither company fared well after the outbreak of the Second World War.

After Balanchine left de Basil's company, he came to the United States upon special invitation by Lincoln Kirstein, the famous American patron of

The Neoclassical ballerina

ballet. Balanchine founded the School of American Ballet in 1934. In the U.S. he felt that he would be able to create "something new from something very basic." He was greatly influenced by the American sense of democracy, and abolished the star system of the old European ballet companies. Even today Balanchine's dancers in the New York City Ballet are listed alphabetically. Though his ballets have specific parts for the corps de ballet, the soloists and the principal dancers, it is not uncommon for a soloist or even a member of the corps to dance a lead role.

Balanchine rejected Fokine's definition of ballet, and returned to the classical style of Petipa and Ivanov. Ignoring the pantomime element in the Russian classics, he studied only the pure dance sequences and developed what is usually defined as a neoclassical style. Like the Russian critic André Levinson, Balanchine maintains that ballet is pure dance, inspired by the music. Thus when the music is classical (*Symphony in C,* by Bizet), the movements in his ballets are balanced, elegant and precise, but when the music is modern (*Agon,* by Stravinsky), the movements are inverted and strangely accented.

Balanchine's New York City Ballet, which grew out of various earlier and smaller companies, was formed in 1948, with its home at the City Center. In 1964, the company moved to luxurious new quarters at the New York State

Theater in Lincoln Center. Balanchine has trained many famous American dancers. In his reputed preference for ballerinas, he follows in the footsteps of Petipa.

The American Ballet Theater, rival of the New York City Ballet, developed out of the Mordkin Ballet, created by Pavlova's partner Michel Mordkin. The company was formed in 1940 with strong financial backing from Lucia Chase, who had studied with Mordkin. In general, ABT has followed the star system, which Balanchine has so energetically rejected, and has featured great American and foreign artists.

Ballet in Russia passed through some difficult moments after many great dancers left, first to join Diaghilev's company in Paris and then to escape the 1917 Revolution. After an initial rejection of ballet as an obsolete art form, reminiscent of czarist decadence, the new Soviet regime accepted ballet as an important part of Russia's cultural heritage. The new ballets were often instruments for political propaganda, but eventually the classics regained their place.

Today ballet is still taught in state-run schools, which produce fine dancers for the various companies—the most famous being the Bolshoi Ballet in Moscow and the Kirov Ballet in Leningrad. The Soviet system differs from those in America and Europe because it guarantees the dancers steady work, a graduated salary and excellent retirement benefits. Most important of all, it represents a direct link with the past. The continuity of Russian ballet is its strength, but at the same time its weakness. This illustrious heritage often stifles fresh experimentation. In recent years, however, the Soviet ballet companies have been exposed to different, sometimes unorthodox, ideas through foreign tours and cultural exchange programs.

* * *

After this brief look at the background of ballet, it may be more difficult than ever to answer the original question of what is ballet. Perhaps its most important characteristic is adaptability. Ballet has survived and come down to us because it has conformed to man's varying artistic preferences. More often than not, the tastes of one generation have been violently condemned by the next, but among the contradictions and the criticisms, ballet continued to develop—not in a vertical sense, but rather in a parallel one. While the relationship between ballet and life may not always be as clear as the situation during the Romantic age, it always exists, albeit in a disguised fashion. Even Balanchine, who so vehemently denies any connections between ballet and real life, maintains that his ballets deal only with *now*. He does not care if these ballets are preserved, since he feels that they will have no significant meaning for the future.

And so all we can do is formulate a definition that describes what ballet has been or what it is right now. We can only guess as to what ballet will be like tomorrow. Future generations will have to take care of themselves and their ballet, just as past generations have done before them.

Chapter 2

The Body
and the Basic
Ballet Positions

Americans, and New Yorkers in particular, are not as attuned to "people-watching" as many of their European cousins. There are, of course, many reasons to explain this difference. Most Americans never walk anywhere, except possibly to the mailbox up the street. Instead they prefer to hop into their cars and get where they are going fast! City dwellers are an exception to this generalization, but they walk briskly, just stopping every so often to glance at an interesting window display, but rarely to admire a pretty pair of legs or a smartly dressed executive. Certainly neither our cities nor our suburbs lend themselves to the pleasurable pastime of people-watching. The distances in America are enormous, and there are just twenty-four hours in every day. Outdoor cafés are hard to find and often uncomfortably noisy. Who wants to sit and watch the traffic race by? Though Americans find time for a quick drink with friends at their favorite bar, they would probably feel awkward sipping the very same drink in the bright sunshine. And they might even be embarrassed to watch all the different people walk by. Somehow or other, we Americans seem to do our relaxing in dark, intimate places where people are safely cloaked in shadows. But not everybody feels this way.

After soccer, people-watching is probably the most popular Italian sport. The handsome young men who loll casually around the countless cafés and girl-watch are indeed trying to live up to their reputation as irresistible Latin lovers. As they sip a chilled *aperitivo,* they vie with one another in their loud, lusty appraisals of every presentable—and even not so presentable—female who happens to wander by. Not-so-young men and once-upon-a-time-young men also participate in this national sport, which apparently has no age restrictions. Or sex restrictions, for that matter, since Italian women are also avid people-watchers. You can feel them stare at you, at your shoes, your jeans, your make-up or whatever, as you walk down those narrow streets. If you stare back at them—and you would probably feel very rude, because we have been taught that staring is impolite—they are not in the least embarrassed. They might even smile at you, while they continue to stare.

There are Americans who like to people-watch. Some may do so surreptitiously so that they will not be caught, so to speak, in the act. Others are more courageous. Dancers, in particular, adore people-watching, and are notoriously critical about it. After all those long years of training, they have become accustomed to looking at bodies, analyzing them and criticizing them. If you want to hear exactly how skillful they are, just sit near a group of dancers—professionals or students, it does not really matter—and listen to their comments on the performance they just saw, on the class they just took or simply on the people strolling by. Cutting, catty, cruel, but always exasperatingly precise in pinpointing defects.

*   *   *

The body is the instrument for dance, and therefore must conform to a series of rigid rules. The instrument is composed of various separate components, each of which has to function both independently and as part of the unit. When all these separate parts work together harmoniously, we may speak of beautiful body coordination. In addition, these separate parts must satisfy certain aesthetic criteria, so that the visual effect they produce is pleasing to the viewer. In other words, the dancer's body must be superbly trained but also beautiful to watch. Right from the early stages of training, a dancer learns what constitutes a beautiful body, and thereafter strives painfully to make his or her own body conform to those requirements.

What is a perfect body for dance? First of all, we must limit our discussion to ballet, since the criteria for a ballerina are different from those for a belly dancer or a flamenco artist. Generally speaking, there are no specific limitations on height except those imposed by specific parts in certain ballets. Swanilda in *Coppélia* (original choreography by Saint-Léon in 1870 to music by Délibes) should be danced by a tiny, doll-like girl, while the Siren in *The Prodigal Son* (original choreography by Balanchine in 1929 to music by Prokofiev) was specifically created for a very tall, long-legged dancer. Furthermore, some choreographers have their own personal preferences about the sizes and shapes of their dancers. Though Balanchine has a definite penchant for tall, willowy blondes, he has not ignored brunettes and medium-height girls.

Ideally a ballerina should be neither too short nor too tall, so that she can dance almost every part. If a dancer is very short, on stage she may appear too sweet and young for an intensely dramatic role. If, however, she is very tall, she may look too statuesque for a lyrical, romantic adagio, especially if her partner is short. No matter how brilliant her technique, the spell of great love is inevitably broken when the princess towers a head above her prince. Every ballerina grows several inches as soon as she stands on toe! Therefore, the problem of height can hardly be ignored.

Today a ballerina should be thin because a lean body corresponds to our idea of beauty. In the past, however, ballerinas often tended to be pleasingly plump. (Poor Madeleine Guimard was nicknamed the "Skeleton of the Graces" because her scrawny figure lacked the voluptuous curves of her rivals.) In addition to our modern preference for the thin look, dancing is easier for both the ballerina and for her partner (who has to lift, carry and throw her) when the girl is thin. Many of today's costumes, especially in modern ballets, are very revealing and show every ounce of extra fat. The lighting on stage adds pounds to even the thinnest wisp of a girl; it is usual to calculate an eight-to-ten-pound apparent weight gain. Worst of all, these "optical" pounds usually land on the more muscular areas, like the thighs or calves. And no ballerina wants big, muscular legs!

Not all girls are lucky enough to have the long, thin legs that are every ballerina's dream. In addition to dieting, there are various theatrical tricks to make the legs appear longer. For example, a few inches can be gained if the leotard is rolled up as high as possible on the sides. If a dancer has short legs, a good costume designer reduces the circumference of the tutu and attaches the twelve layers of the skirt higher on the hips in order to give the illusion of longer limbs.

A foot with a high instep improves the line of a dancer's leg movements. Though beautifully arched feet may be lovely to admire, they are constitutionally weaker because of their flexibility; therefore, the girl with the beautiful insteps has to work much harder to build up the tremendous strength required for toe work. It actually takes her longer to rise up on toe because she has to roll over farther!

Sloping shoulders give the neck a lovely, long line and add a touch of distinction to the arm movements. A girl with square, broad shoulders has to be very careful to keep her shoulders down when dancing, otherwise she will seem to have no neck, or a very short one. Raised shoulders will also tend to make her arm movements look strong and angular.

A full bosom may be the answer to every actress's prayer, but not so for ballerinas. Scantily cut bodices plus lots of writhing can cause visibly embarrassing situations on stage. Doubly embarrassing because the ballerina only imagines the audience's reactions, but she can actually hear the zesty comments by the dancers and stagehands in the wings.

The larger the dancer's head, the taller she appears on stage. A full face can be corrected quite easily with proper make-up and careful hair-styling. A tall girl should never wear her hair in a high bun, unless she wishes to appear three inches taller than the rest of the ballet company.

*   *   *

Ballet is unnatural! It represents the victory of the body over nature. A dancer must carefully and painfully train her body for years so she can transcend its natural limitations. Thus perfection for the dancer means dehumanizing the body.

The natural position of the body is relaxed—head looking forward, spine more or less straight, stomach and buttocks muscles lax, arms hanging down the sides, legs and feet pointing straight ahead with the knees slightly bent. There are, of course, innumerable variations on this natural theme—the spine curved and the pelvis pushed forward so that the shoulders are rounded, or the spine overarched and the shoulders pulled back to create the sway-back look. In ballet, however, there is only one correct stance. The spine should be erect, and the rib cage expanded and pulled upward. The strength of this position comes from the stomach and buttocks muscles as well as a strong back. This "invisible" strength allows the torso, neck and head to appear relaxed, without even a hint of muscular strain. The arms, when raised, move softly and effortlessly from the shoulder blades rather than from the shoulders. Even when fully extended, the arms are always slightly bent at the elbow.

The mention of body placement makes me remember my first class at the School of American Ballet. I was only fourteen and had just been placed in the B, or intermediate, class. The practice room felt big and strange, all the faces seemed vaguely hostile. Being the "new girl" from New Jersey, I knew that all those New York eyes would be watching me in the mirrors. As I nervously did a few warm-up stretches, a sweet, gray-haired lady in a long skirt floated into the room. Everyone snapped to attention. During the exercises at the barre, this sweet lady came over to me, smiled graciously as she welcomed me to the school, stuck her fingers gently yet firmly into my stomach and back and miraculously popped my body into place. "This, my dear, is how you should stand," she whispered, "because this position will make you dance."

It was only after class that I learned who this lady was. She was Muriel Stuart, Anna Pavlova's protégée. I realized how lucky I was to be able to study with someone who had actually known the great Pavlova. In my own young way, I felt suddenly immersed in the great ballet tradition.

The real innovation of body placement in ballet is the turnout. Instead of pointing forward in the natural position, the feet and legs are turned to the side, so that they form a 180-degree angle. This "turned out" position actually starts at the hips, which must be "opened" so that the legs and feet can point to the sides. As we have seen, the turnout in ballet developed with the introduction of the raised stage; since the audience could see the dancers only from the front, the steps had to be adjusted. Side-to-side motion with feet turned out at, originally, a 45-degree angle enabled the dancers to move gracefully while it allowed the audience to see all the movements. Through the years, the turnout was opened wider and wider until it reached the 180-degree angle. Unnatural as it may feel to the beginning student, the turnout is still the foundation of classical ballet.

Young dancers have to be trained gradually to develop the turnout. The great ballet reformer Noverre used special orthopedic devices to improve his pupils' turnout. Today this method might not meet with parental approval. Forcing a young student to strain his muscles in a turnout can be dangerous since the body lacks the necessary flexibility in the early stages of training. To compensate, a student may "cheat" by turning in her knees when she does a plié (a slight bending of the knees) or by rolling over on her big toe. This bad habit can cause bunions. A good teacher should never push students beyond their limitations or allow any type of muscular cheating.

Understanding correct body placement is fundamental to ballet. It is customary to encourage beginning students to check themselves in the mirrors that cover one wall of the practice room. Unless a student can see and feel her mistakes in body placement, she will never master the technique of keeping the correct body placement as she moves. It is not the correct body alignment per se that is difficult, so much as the rapid succession of adjustments that have to be made when one dances. These delicate shifts require tremendous muscle control.

The positions in classical ballet have been developed through the centuries. The first mention of dance positions for the feet is found in *Orchésographie,* an interesting book published in 1588 by a priest who used the pseudonym Thoinot Arbeau. This work contained a detailed study of the court dances of the day and referred to three specific positions for the feet. Raoul Feuillet described the five positions that are currently used in classical ballet in his book *Choréographie;* he also emphasized the importance of the turnout. According to P. Rameau in *Le Maître à Danser,* published in 1725, it was Beauchamps (Louis XIV's dancing teacher, a famous dancer and choreographer in his own right) who invented the five positions. In all probability, Beauchamps simply codified the dancing technique of his day.

Today there are five positions in classical ballet. A position is defined as the specific placement of the legs when both feet are on the ground. It goes without saying that the correct body placement must be observed in all the positions.

In first position, the heels of both feet touch, and the toes are turned outward to form a 180-degree angle. Ballet teachers should always begin with this position since it clearly illustrates the importance of the turnout. Beginning students, who must never be forced to overstrain their muscles as they attempt to master the turnout, should be aware of a twinge of muscle strain, but never pain.

Second position maintains the 180-degree angle of first position, but there should be a space—usually the length of one foot—between the heels. Second position is used specifically for exercises on the barre (the wooden bar attached to the wall for the warm-up exercises), such as the demi- and grand pliés, or as a preparatory and landing position for certain turns.

Third position, used very rarely, is halfway between first and fifth. Both feet are completely turned out at a 180-degree angle, but the heel of one foot touches the instep of the other so that the legs are slightly crossed. Beginners, who have difficulty in forming a correct fifth position, often use third as a substitute.

In fourth position, the feet are again placed at a 180-degree angle, but the heel of the front foot is positioned directly in front of the toe of the back foot. The two feet are separated by the length of one foot. Fourth position is commonly used as a preparatory and landing position for many turns as well as for rapid movements where it would be almost impossible to end in fifth position.

Fifth position is the most important for classical ballet. The easiest way to form a fifth is to turn out the feet into first position and then to slide one foot directly in front of the other till the toe of the front foot touches the heel of the back foot. The legs are of course crossed. Practically all ballet steps start from fifth position, because the dancer has a stronger "push-off" from fifth than from the other positions. The complete turnout and correct body placement are very difficult in fifth position. A student will never master ballet technique unless fifth position becomes second nature to her.

The neoclassical reformers have invented two new positions, which have not met with great success. The so-called sixth position is nothing more than the natural position—that is, both feet placed side by side with the toes pointing directly to the front. In ballet, sixth position must be combined with the correct body placement, or else the dancer would look like a tired housewife waiting in a long line at the supermarket. Sixth position is used in modern ballets.

Seventh position is actually a variation on fourth.[1] Here the dancer must stand in fourth position on toe—not vertically, in the so-called classical toe position, but pushed over till she is actually standing on her toenails. This "neoclassical" toe position is rarely used.

In classical ballet, the arms form a very important part of the total movement. They add grace and elegance to the body. In general, classical ballet avoids harsh, angular lines, and strives to achieve flowing, effortless movement. The soft, almost relaxed arm movements should contrast with the brilliant technique of the feet and legs. This is, however, one of the most difficult parts of ballet training, because the arms and shoulders tend to tense when all the other muscles are strained. Therefore, students have to learn to use their arms correctly from the beginning. Even though they may not be able to coordinate arms, legs and feet perfectly, they should be aware that ballet requires the harmonious functioning of all the parts of the body. Sparkling footwork alone makes only a classroom dancer, not a ballerina.

The beginning student learns that there are five positions of the arms to correspond to the five positions of the legs and feet.[2] In first position, the arms are gently curved in front of the chest until the fingertips almost touch. The arms should be held slightly lower than shoulder level, so that they seem to slope down from the shoulders. This position softens what would otherwise be an angular line, while it adds length to the neck.

In second position, both arms are extended to the sides and held directly over the feet. Here again they are placed a little lower than the shoulders. By extended, I do not mean taut, but rather slightly curved. The upper arm should be held high, parallel to the ground, while the forearm and hand gently curve. The fingers should be relaxed, with the thumb held close to the hand; sometimes the two center fingers are slightly lower than the index and little fingers.[3] If the fingers are too stiff, the hand appears tense and strained; if the fingers are too relaxed, the hand appears droopy and inexpressive.

In third position, one arm remains extended to the side, while the other is raised over the head—not directly over, but slightly in front, so as to frame the face. Since third position of the legs may be done with the right or the left foot front, either the right or the left arm may be raised.

For fourth position, one arm is kept over the head, while the other arm is curved in front of the chest. Here again, the right or the left arm is raised.

There are two kinds of fifth position for the arms. In the high fifth position, both arms are raised above the head to frame the face. Here students must be careful not to raise their shoulders; instead they must hold them down by pinching the shoulder blades together. As the shoulders are pulled down, the neck and head should be pulled up. In the low fifth position, the arms are curved in front of the pelvis. Here, as in first position, the fingers are almost touching.

The positions of the head are also very important. The usual position is the tête de face, or head facing forward. The shoulders are pulled down, while the chin is slightly raised and the eyes look forward. Generally a ballerina keeps her lips slightly parted in a very small smile, which minimizes any sign of strain and enables her to breathe more easily. Since ballet demands tremendous endurance, students must learn to control their breathing as they dance. The slight smile is one trick to keep them from running out of breath in difficult, winding combinations. The other common position of the head is de profil (to the side, or profile), which is a favorite for the adagio.

In addition to the de face and de profil positions, the head may be bent forward (tête penchée en avant). This position is sometimes used when a dancer begins a combination or when a male dancer bows. It also expresses emotions such as fear, shame or humility in pantomime sequences. The head thrown backward (tête penchée en arrière) is used in steps that involve backbends (cambré).

Beginning students should practice the basic positions of the legs, feet and arms with the head facing forward. Next they may occasionally turn the head to the side, as they switch arms and legs from one position to another. After they have mastered this fundamental technique, they learn the various positions of the torso, which can move independently while the hips remain in place. Generally the torso faces directly front—that is, de face—but sometimes it may be turned to form an angle with the hips. This is the épaulé, or shouldered, position. Occasionally the torso is bent sideway (penché de côté), forward (penché en avant) or backward (penché en arrière), but these positions are used mainly in the port de bras au corps cambré (movement of the arms which accompanies the torso as it bends forward, sideward or backward). Classical ballet forbids the ensellé, or saddled, position, whereby the back is hollowed as the hips are thrust forward to compensate the shift of weight. This position is used in many kinds of ethnic dances, however.

The five basic positions are first learned with both feet on the ground, but they may also be performed on one foot. They are called demi-positions, or half positions, when the toe of the free foot only touches the floor. They become positions dérivées, or derivative positions, when the free leg is extended in the air; the leg may be either à la demi-hauteur (or half height—that is, below the waist, usually about midcalf level) or à la hauteur (full height, with the leg at waist level or higher). The free leg may also be raccourci, or bent, most commonly in the passé or the attitude.

The basic positions are important because they define the official poses in

a

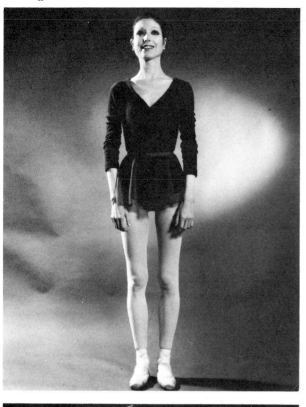

b

e

f

c

d

The "natural" body position and the five basic ballet positions: (a) The "natural" position; (b) Feet and arms in first position; (c) Feet and arms in second position; (d) Feet and arms in third position; (e) Feet and arms in fourth position; (f) Feet and arms in high fifth position; (g) Feet and arms in low fifth position

g

ballet. Alone they do not create ballet, because they are basically stationary. Ballet, like all other forms of dance, involves movement from one pose to another. In order for the basic positions of the legs, feet, torso, arms and head to become ballet, they must incorporate movement. In classical ballet, there are seven ways to move: to bend (*plier*), to stretch (*étendre*), to raise (*relever*), to slide (*glisser*), to jump (*sauter*), to dart (*élancer*) and to turn (*tourner*). Only by combining these basic positions into moving sequences does the student begin to dance.

Genevieve Guillot and Germaine Prudhommeau, authors of *The Book of Ballet,* have calculated the possible combinations of all the ballet positions. The total number of positions is forty-seven, subdivided as follows: twenty-six positions of the legs, seven positions of the torso, seven positions of the arms and seven positions of the head. It is possible to combine these forty-seven positions in 13,284 ways. These can then be performed in three different ways: with the foot flat on the ground (à plat), with the foot on half toe (sur la demi-pointe) or with the foot on toe (sur la pointe). Thus the total number of possibilities reaches 39,852. If we allowed a dancer two seconds to execute each possible position, it would take her twenty-two hours, eight minutes and twenty-four seconds to run through them all.

But the surprises do not end here. The possibilities become astronomical if we add movement—that is, the transition from one pose to another. In this case, the possible combinations reach an astounding 1,588,181,904! If a dancer had five seconds to go through each of these possibilities, it would take her 250 years to perform all these theoretical steps! Interesting but not very practical, since some people in the audience find even two hours of ballet too long for comfort!

Leaving aside these theoretical considerations, we could consider the basic positions as the letters in the alphabet of ballet. In themselves they have no meaning until they are combined into words and then the words into sentences. The balletic words are the separate steps that the student learns to master, first on the barre and then in the center of the room. Next she forms these words into balletic sentences, or combinations. This is the real challenge, because she has to coordinate everything she has learned thus far. Only then does she really begin to dance. These combinations are far more than technical precision drills. They actually speak to her, and convey a message to the viewer. After all, ballet is body language!

Chapter 3

The Barre Is Not a Bar!

Many people are quite surprised to learn that all ballet dancers, even the great stars, have to do the very same warm-up exercises as beginning students. "But after all those years of practice," they insist, "isn't a professional too good for all that routine?" The answer is a sharp no. A dancer, like an athlete, never forgets those strenuous warm-up exercises, no matter how tired she may be. Failure to do them often results in injuries, which may even be permanent.

In addition to the risk of injury, there are other important reasons why dancers must practice regularly. First of all, the muscles quickly weaken and lose their flexibility unless they are worked on a daily basis. Secondly, the muscles, along with the rest of the body, grow old. Depressing as it may be, this inevitable process of deterioration starts after the magic age of twenty-one! While muscle aging is all but imperceptible to the average person, dancers can feel the difference. Teena confesses that today it is harder for her to get back into shape than it was six or eight years ago. She explains that during a layoff her muscles stiffen more quickly, and consequently she has to work longer and harder to loosen them up. "But I still have a few more good years left before I retire," she hastens to add. "We dancers are more conscious, perhaps even more afraid, of aging, so we tend to take better care of ourselves." Indeed, according to legend, dancers never grow old!

The time a dancer spends on muscle maintenance is a long-term investment which enables her to perform many years after she has passed her muscular prime. Interestingly enough, most ballerinas reach their peak at about thirty. Though they achieve the technical virtuosity to perform the most challenging steps before that time, they usually lack the emotional maturity and experience that gives "soul" to their dancing. Not every dancer, however, has the physical and psychological stamina to adhere to the rigid ballet schedule and make all the necessary sacrifices.

Proper warm-up and daily practice also enable the professional dancer to perfect small technical points and to strengthen weak spots. For performance, a dancer must concentrate on the total effect she produces. She must dance with her body and her soul, and consequently must overlook technical details. Unless she spends some time refreshing her technique, however, she may develop poor, sloppy habits that will eventually weaken her technical skill. When a dancer cannot take class, she will work out by herself for an hour or so. Many professional dancers tape music, so they can do their own workout. Teena admits that one of the most grueling aspects of ballet practice is warming up without music. "Even the simplest movement is torture. That's why I always take my transistor radio on tour. It's sometimes fun to use Elton John for pliés and progressive country for grands battements."

Thus the ballerina can never forget the classroom, where she started out many years before. The class is a ritual for her. It is a technical and spiritual return to ballet basics, and, as such, revitalizes her. No dancer is complete unless she leaves the classroom and dances on stage; no dancer, however, remains complete unless she remembers to leave the stage and return periodically to the classroom.

*   *   *

The typical ballet classroom is a rectangular studio with barres[1] (wooden or metal poles attached to the wall about four feet from the ground) on three walls and mirrors on the fourth. During the first part of the class, the dancers hold on to the barre, generally with one hand, and perform a variety of exercises to both sides. Though the students should "feel" the proper body positions for all the exercises, they can double-check them in the mirrors. The floor should be made of wood, never concrete or wood over concrete. A hard floor strains the dancers' legs and builds up knotty muscles.

Though many new classrooms are air-conditioned, dancers generally prefer the stifling older studios, which would make the average person feel as if he were standing on the equator. Dancers adore heat, because their muscles stay

warm and limber. They bundle themselves up with woolen leg warmers, rubber pants and fleecy shirts to make themselves sweat. They are used to high temperatures because of the tremendous physical exertion in their work and the heat from spotlights. An outdoor stage on a damp summer evening or a poorly heated, drafty theater will inevitably create crises among the dancers, and sometimes even compromise the success of the performance.

A ballet class lasts anywhere from one to two hours, with one and a half hours the usual length for intermediate or advanced students. Approximately half the class time is spent at the barre, so that the student can warm up the muscles and learn or review the basic steps in the language of ballet. The aim of the barre is to acquire perfection through concentration on the fundamental details. The various muscles are isolated and exercised separately in order to build up the strength and control that are needed to combine these details into meaningful dance phrases. In the search for perfection, however, the body is dehumanized and purged, as it were, of its earthly limitations. Right from the first class, the dancer is taught that she must strain to transcend the physical laws of gravity. The body, like the soul, must soar upward.

The exercises, with a few exceptions, are generally done first with one hand on the barre, and then repeated to the opposite side. Support from the barre enables the beginner to perform exercises that would otherwise be technically too difficult; it allows the professional to concentrate specifically on tiny technical flaws. A good teacher must be very careful not to permit students to hang on to the barre "for dear life" or to use it as a real prop. The student should hold the barre lightly with her fingertips, and should theoretically be able to let go at any moment without losing her balance.

Many years ago, when I was an intermediate student at the School of American Ballet, Mr. Oboukhoff, one of the most colorful of the old Russian teachers, would periodically check our balance. As he stalked around the room, he would casually step behind someone and then—sometimes, not always—pull her hand off the barre. The first time he did this to me, I nearly fell over. "Ah, ah, Big Miss"—that was his special name for me because I was very tall, but also because he could not pronounce Joan—"no good, no good," he bellowed in his guttural Russian-English. "Vat you do? You fall? You *no* dance!" As I gazed at him in terror, he started to laugh! Maybe at me, or maybe at his own joke, but I was too embarrassed to care. Though I may not have perfected my body placement, I never got caught off balance again—at least in his class!

Although there is no fixed order for the barre exercises in the Russian and French schools (the Cecchetti method is more rigid), most teachers follow a similar pattern, and spend from thirty to forty minutes on the barre. A good teacher carefully organizes the exercises to minimize muscular strain and tension. It is particularly important to alternately stretch and relax the muscles in order to avoid cramping, which, in the long run, builds up muscular bulk. For example, a series of exercises with fondus, ronds de jambe en l'air, grands battements and finally a sustained adagio would cause severe cramping in the thigh and calf muscles. If repeated daily, it would eventually produce knotty leg muscles.

While the fundamental exercises on the barre are relatively few, they can be combined into a variety of sequences that meet the students' needs and abilities and at the same time reflect the teacher's personality. The exercises can be done with simple or complex accompanying arm and head movements. At times the individual steps are worked into long, difficult combinations that challenge both the students' technical skill and their memory. It would indeed be unfair to underestimate the importance of a quick mind for ballet. First of all, the terminology is French. Secondly, students must familiarize themselves with all the new steps and their names. Finally, many teachers demonstrate a combination only once and only to one side. The students are expected to do the combination perfectly on the first run-through, and are often required to reverse it.

*   *   *

The plié (from the French *plier,* "to bend"), a bending of one or both knees, is a fundamental step in all forms of dance. It serves as both a preparatory and a landing position for most dance movements. When a dancer starts a jumping or turning sequence with a plié, she has a stronger push-off. It is far easier to end a step with a plié than with straight legs because the plié absorbs, so to speak, the momentum that has been built up. A dancer should always end her jumps with a plié as a precautionary measure. Landing with straight knees can cause serious injuries, especially to the Achilles tendon.

Demi-plié

The plié in classical ballet must respect correct body placement and turn-out. The plié may be performed in every position, but on the barre, third position is usually eliminated. There are two kinds of pliés. In the demi-plié, the dancer bends both knees as much as she can, but does not raise her heels from the ground. Beginners must be careful not to cheat in a demi-plié and raise their heels, though some professional dancers do not always put their heels down. The sequences are often so rapid that there is no time for a perfect demi-plié. And there are professionals who feel that their dancing control improves when they do *not* put down their heels in demi-plié for jumps.

To perform the grand plié, the dancer starts with a demi-plié and then slowly deepens the bend until the thighs are horizontal. In the grand plié, the heels are raised, but only at the last possible moment. The longer the dancer presses her heels into the floor, the more she stretches her Achilles tendon. The bending and straightening movement in both demi- and grand pliés should be flowing. Jerky movement can cause muscle strain. As soon as the maximum bend in the grand plié is reached, the dancer should immediately start to straighten her knees. She must never "sit" in a grand plié; aside from the unpleasant visual effect, this would tend to build up thick thigh muscles.

A ballet class inevitably starts with plié exercises to stretch the muscles, joints and Achilles tendons. The more supple and flexible the muscles and tendons, the deeper the plié. A good plié is important for a dancer because it momentarily allows the muscles to relax before the next sequence. A plié also develops a dancer's sense of balance, and enables her to move quickly and without effort from one step to the next.

On the barre, the plié exercises are usually done with accompanying arm movements to develop greater body coordination. The downward movement of the arm must be perfectly timed with the bending of the knees. This means that when the dancer reaches the maximum of the plié, her free arm should be down, gently curved in front of the pelvis in a low fifth position. As soon as she starts to straighten her knees, the arm should begin its upward movement. Although the plié may at first seem like an exercise specifically designed for the legs, it actually involves coordination of the entire body.

The next exercises on the barre are usually variations of the battement tendu (from the French *battement,* "beating," and *tendu,* "stretched"). For a battement tendu, the working leg—the leg away from the barre—slides out from first or fifth position with the toe brushing the floor. The leg must always be kept straight and well turned out from the hip. When the leg is completely extended, the toe should be neatly pointed, adding grace to the line of the movement, but also strengthening the foot. When a dancer jumps, she pushes off from the plié by pointing her toes and straightening her knees. A strong pointed toe helps build up the tremendous strength needed for toe work.

The battements tendus are usually done en croix—that is, to the fourth position front, to the second position, to the fourth position back, and then to the second position, or vice versa. Battements tendus may be done with or without a plié. If they are done quickly, the working leg is extended briskly,

Grand plié with arms in second position

Starting position for battement tendu   *Battement tendu to second position*

with the toe slightly leaving the floor, and then pulled back in. This version, the battement tendu jeté, is very helpful for strengthening the toes and increasing the flexibility of the ankle joints.

Generally the accent of the battement tendu is "in"—that is, the movement begins and concludes in fifth or first position. Occasionally the battement tendu can be done with the accent "out," whereby the movement begins and ends with the toe pointed and the leg extended. For the battement tendu exercises, the free arm is usually held to the side.

The rond de jambe à terre is a circular movement in which the pointed toe describes a semicircle on the floor. If the rond de jambe à terre is done dehors, or outward, the foot starts from the fourth position to the front, moves to the second and then on to the fourth back. As the foot passes through first position, the heel is lowered slowly to the floor. The rond de jambe à terre en dedans is a backward semicircular movement starting from the fourth position back. This exercise is particularly important for developing the turnout, strengthening the pointed toe and increasing flexibility in the hip joint. The leg must move as a unit from the hip, but the hip remains stationary. One of the most difficult, yet elementary, rules of ballet is that the hips remain immobile, while the legs, arms, head and upper body move.

At the end of the rond de jambe à terre sequence, it is customary to return to the fifth position. The upper torso is bent forward (penché en avant), with the free arm moving from the side into a low fifth position. The spine must be held straight. When the dancer has bent down as far as she can, she relaxes her neck and lets her head drop forward. As she slowly raises her torso, the free arm should pass through the first position and then up to a high fifth position. She usually bends backward (penché en arrière) and drops her head back. As she lifts her torso, the free arm returns to the second position.

The battement fondu is an exercise that develops muscle control, turnout and balance. It is particularly important for girls because it improves extension—a dancer's ability to hold the extended leg as high as possible in the air. The battement fondu usually starts with the working leg pointed to the side. The standing leg bends into a plié as the working leg moves into the sur le cou-de-pied devant position (here the foot of the working leg is wrapped around the ankle of the standing leg, so that the heel sticks out in front of the ankle and the toe is pointed down toward the back of the ankle). Then the working leg is extended (développé) to the fourth front, to the second or to the fourth back. The leg may be low (à la demi-hauteur) or high (à la hauteur). As the working leg is extended, the dancer may stand à plat (with the foot flat on the ground), move to the demi-pointe (half toe) or rise to the pointe (toe).

Penché en arrière with feet in fourth position

The battement frappé is a rapid, sharply accented movement which aims at strengthening the ankles, toes and calves for jumps. The dancer usually starts with the working leg pointed to the second. The foot is brought to the sur le cou-de-pied position, and briskly extended to the fourth front, to the second or to the fourth back. As the leg is extended, the ball of the foot should hit the floor, and then the toe should be strongly pointed. The battement frappé can be done with the working leg straight, in plié, à plat, on pointe or on demi-pointe. There also exists a battement frappé double, whereby the working foot passes from the sur le cou-de-pied derrière (here the heel leans against the back of the ankle of the working leg and the pointed toe is held away from the ankle), to the sur le cou-de-pied devant and then into the frappé movement with the leg. For the battement frappé en croix, the starting position of each frappé must be adjusted accordingly—that is, the dancer passes from the sur le cou-de-pied derrière to the sur le cou-de-pied devant for the frappé in fourth position front, but from the sur le cou-de-pied devant to the sur le cou-de-pied derrière for the frappé to the second, and so forth.

After a series of battements frappés, it is usual to do battement sur le cou-de-pied in order to prepare the dancer for the batterie, or beaten steps, that will be done off barre. In this exercise, the dancer places her working foot in the sur le cou-de-pied devant position, and rapidly moves it from the front to the back. The standing leg may be à plat, sur la demi-pointe or sur la pointe. This exercise usually concludes with the battement battu, in which the working foot starts in the sur le cou-de-pied position devant or derrière and beats against the ankle of the standing leg. Battement battu is usually performed on pointe or demi-pointe.

For the rond de jambe en l'air, the working leg is extended to the second position and forms a small circle in the air by rotating the lower leg from the knee. The hip and thigh must be kept securely in place. The circle may be outward (en dehors) or inward (en dedans). The leg is usually held at waist level (à la hauteur), so that the toe brushes the knee of the supporting leg as it describes the circle. If the rond de jambe en l'air is done à la demi-hauteur, the toe brushes the calf rather than the knee. This exercise is extremely difficult, and requires tremendous control of the leg muscles. The leg must be kept at the same height, and should *never* drop or flop during the circular movement. The rond de jambe en l'air is important for the turn sequences that the ballerina has to perform with her partner.

Preparation to the side for a battement fondu

The plié movement in battement fondu

The développé movement in battement fondu

Sur le cou-de-pied

The grands battements, or high kicks, are commonly used in many dance forms. In ballet, the grand battement must be performed in accordance with the strict rules of body placement and turnout. As the dancer kicks her leg to the various positions, her toe must be neatly pointed, her knee kept straight and her hips held stationary. In some of the modern ballets, however, the rigid classical laws are forgotten, and the dancer is allowed to let her body follow the thrust of the leg. The effect is spectacular, but the lines of classical ballet are compromised.

The grand battement may be done en croix or en cloche (here the leg swings from the fourth front to the fourth back in a bell-like movement). The body should remain erect. For the grand battement en balançoire, the body leans backward as the leg is kicked to the front, and then moves forward as the leg is kicked to the back.

The adagio (from the Italian *ad agio,* meaning "at ease") is a series of slow, flowing movements. It is perhaps the most important movement at the barre, because it combines most of the preceding exercises in a sustained sequence that requires tremendous muscle control. The dancer must be particularly careful to keep a graceful, harmonious line as she moves from one step to the next. Balance and muscle control are essential for good adagio work. High extension is important for girls. Practicing the adagio movement on pointe is especially recommended since it helps prepare the girls for adagio work with a partner. The term "adagio" also refers to the opening section of the classical pas de deux, where the ballerina, assisted by her partner, performs elaborate sequences involving développés, grands ronds de jambe en l'air, arabesques, attitudes, slow lifts and many types of pirouettes.

The adagio sequences on barre often start with a passé. Here the dancer bends her working leg, and moves the toe up the supporting leg until it touches the knee. Then the leg may be extended (développé) to the fourth front, carried through the second to the fourth back and held in an arabesque. This circular movement, called the grand rond de jambe en l'air, requires considerable strength, because the dancer must lift her leg higher as she moves from one position to the next. Lowering the leg would spoil the visual harmony of this flowing movement.

One of the most important poses in the adagio is the arabesque. The historical origins of the term remain mysterious, but it would appear that this pose took its name from the Moorish ornamental designs with entwining leaves, flowers and plants. Even as late as the early nineteenth century, "arabesque" referred to intertwined groups of male and female dancers who held flowers and garlands. Carlo Blasis prided himself on being the first to explain the parallel between the arabesque ornamental designs and the picturesque dance patterns. The arabesque as we know it today became popular during the

Grand battement to fourth front

Passé

"golden age of ballet," when Romantic ballerinas stood gracefully on one toe with their back leg extended—waist high only!

Variations on the arabesque are infinite, and differ slightly in the three important schools—Italian, French and Russian. In all the schools, however, the long line of the extended leg is complemented by the extended arms. Generally the back is held erect, but the dancer often uses the spectacular arabesque penchée, where she forces her extended leg higher by bending her torso forward. In a perfect arabesque penchée, the extended leg forms a 180-degree angle with the supporting leg! The arabesque can be done with the working foot à plat, on the demi-pointe or on pointe; arabesques can also be done in demi-plié. In addition to constant practice at the barre, the dancer improves her arabesques with specific stretches that increase the flexibility of the leg muscles and hips.

Although the adagio is usually the last exercise on the barre, some teachers prefer to end with simple relevés—raising the weight from the foot à plat to the pointe or to the demi-pointe. A relevé may be done on one or both feet, with or without plié. Other teachers may add a short combination with little

Arabesque

Arabesque penchée

Relevé

jumps to strengthen the dancers' feet for entrechats (jumps in which the dancer crosses her feet in the air). For girls, a teacher will often end the barre exercises with preparation for fouettés ("fouetté rond de jambe en tournant" is the complete name). This spectacular turn has been immortalized in the third act of *Swan Lake,* where Odile (the Black Swan) performs thirty-two fouettés. For the fouetté, the ballerina turns on one leg, propelled by the circular whipping movement of the extended leg, usually held at waist level. She must remain in the same place and must not "travel" all over the floor. The dancer gains additional momentum from both the whipping arm movement, which parallels that of the legs, and the snapping of her head as she turns.

* * *

The steps discussed represent only the skeleton of the barre exercises. They can be combined into infinite sequences of varying length and complexity. The barre is important because it enables the dancer to work on detail, correct mistakes, improve turnout and, above all, consolidate body placement. With the added support from the barre, the dancer can concentrate on specific muscles and strengthen her weak spots. Careful exercises on the barre improve the dancer's footwork and correct sickling—rolling the weight toward the little or big toe instead of concentrating it on the ball of the foot.

At the end of the barre exercises, the dancers are all perspiring profusely and mopping their glistening brows with towels. Before they move out into the center, they bend over to catch their breath or retie their shoes. Many stretch out on the floor to limber their muscles before they move to the challenge of the off barre exercises. Off barre is always more exciting—though not necessarily more important—than the barre, because this is when the students first begin to dance.

Chapter 4

Stretching
Your Muscles

Dancers are very special people who often do very special things. Sometimes this very special behavior can turn other people off because they lack the acute body awareness that has become second nature to dancers after years of specialized training. Undoubtedly it can be irritating to be near people who have to flex their muscles, crack their hip joints or massage their calves every ten minutes. "Are all these contortions really necessary," queries the casual observer, "or is it just an attention-getting gimmick?"

Stiffness is one of the most frequent problems that plague dancers. Though their muscles get stiff from too much work—morning class plus four to five hours of rehearsal, followed by a hard performance—these very same muscles can also tighten up from too little work. Lack of movement can be voluntary or involuntary, depending on the circumstances.

It goes without saying that every once in a while, a dancer is entitled to a short vacation. Rest revitalizes the body, but perhaps most important of all, it lets those poor, overworked muscles just relax and do nothing. The result is that the muscles actually shrink. Resting the muscles periodically for a brief spell is an extremely important aspect of a dancer's body maintenance. Continuous overwork increases the risk of injury, and eventually builds up thick, ugly muscular bulk, which is particularly unattractive for the female dancer.

Naturally, the price to pay for this therapeutic rest is stiffness, but it is good stiffness. Teena maintains that after a vacation her dancing actually improves, once she gets herself back into condition. In addition to these longer periods of rest, she always takes a weekly "mini rest." This means that she dances six days a week, and reserves the seventh (usually Monday) as her day of rest.

Involuntary lack of movement is a completely different matter, and is generally caused by factors beyond the dancer's control. Unbroken periods of forced inactivity, such as long rides in cars, buses or planes, produce cramps and general muscle tenseness, which can spoil the evening performance. On bus tours, dancers always clamor for frequent rest stops, so that they can get out and do a few stretches to keep the muscles limber.

The situation on a plane is not much better. Much to the dismay of a seat partner, a dancer will find every excuse to get up and walk down the aisle—another glass of orange juice, more magazines, something to ask the stewardess. Once Teena caused a small scandal on an Alitalia night flight from Kenya to Rome. Since the plane was not full, she was determined to get some sleep without having her muscles cramp up. She wrapped herself in two blankets and stretched out on the floor under the seats. Her unorthodox position shocked the steward, who tried to convince the *signorina* to sit up in her seat like all the other, normal passengers. But the *signorina* was inflexible. She emphatically informed the wide-eyed steward that she was not like all the other passengers because she was a ballerina. And then she turned over on her side, pulled the blanket up to her chin and went to sleep. The poor, bedazzled steward walked away muttering, *"Mamma mia . . . ste donne!"* ("My heavens . . . these women!")

Don't ever go on a ballet charter if you object to dancing in the aisles. Dancers in a group flight have been known to perform stretches, jetés or arabesques just to pass away those long hours or to work off the calories from the airplane lunch. These flights can be a harrowing experience for anyone who does not understand dancers. As I said before, dancers are very special people.

*   *   *

Stretching is a very controversial topic in ballet. There are many theories on how, when, where and why to stretch or not to stretch. Each dancer must find his personal answer to this question. The critics of stretching maintain that ballet exercises at the barre, provided they are performed regularly, keep the muscles supple. In their opinion, stretching is not only superfluous, but

Stretching in arabesque penchée

also potentially dangerous because it can injure some muscles and even reduce a dancer's elevation. The enthusiastic stretching "freaks," however, feel
that the body can never be limber enough. Stretching is imperative because it
increases flexibility and counteracts the rigid body alignment of classical
ballet.

Between these two extremes are the various groups of moderates, who all
agree that some stretching is important, but cannot agree on how much. Some
contend that a dancer should stretch before the barre in order to warm up the
muscles for the ballet exercises. Others, insisting that stretching should never
be done before the class because the risk of injury is higher with cold muscles,
advocate it after the barre exercises, when all the muscles have been individu-
ally warmed up.

Some dancers believe that stretching is purely a personal matter. Only
the individual can regulate the correct amount of pressure or pull. Others
prefer to have someone help them stretch their muscles. They feel that this
extra assistance pushes them beyond their natural limitations.

While ballet still respects traditionally classical tastes, in recent years there
has been greater cooperation between modern dance and ballet. This mutual
recognition reflects a definite improvement in the "diplomatic" relations between the two dance forms. At the beginning of this century, however, the
exponents of modern dance inveighed against what they termed ballet's rigid
and decadent formalism. In their desire to be completely autonomous,
modern dancers tried to forget their debt to ballet, and defined their rival as a
dusty relic from the past. Isadora Duncan, in particular, cried out for freedom
from the bonds of tradition. Technique, she felt, was superfluous since it only
taught a person how to move, not how to dance. Dancing meant expressing
one's inner feelings through spontaneous movement.

Lots of things have changed since Isadora Duncan's time. Today it seems as
if this sibling rivalry is giving way to a new willingness on the part of both
modern and ballet dancers to forget their old misunderstandings. Most
modern dancers now admit that ballet is a superb way to train and discipline
the body, even though they may reject ballet's emphasis on formalism. Many
recent ballets—and even some not so recent ones—clearly show how choreographers have successfully incorporated specific movements of modern dance
into ballet. In 1959, Martha Graham helped Balanchine choreograph *Epi-
sodes* (with music by Webern), which today ranks among his most famous

abstract ballets. In 1966, Merce Cunningham choreographed a balletic version of *Summerspace* for the New York City Ballet. The dancers had some initial difficulty in executing steps that contradicted the rules of classical ballet, but the experiment worked well.

Though the modern ballets are the visible proof of how modern dance has affected ballet, the influence at the theoretical level is even stronger. Perhaps the best examples of this new cooperation can be found in the classroom, particularly in the area of stretches. Ballet is based on certain specific movements which, when performed with proper muscle control and perfect body placement, give the viewer the illusion of effortless movement. While modern dance also respects rules of muscle control and body placement, the range of acceptable movement is much broader than in ballet.

There are two important explanations for this difference. First of all, most modern dancers—it is always dangerous to speak in absolute terms—do not want to create the illusion of effortless movement. Some movements may indeed be effortless, but others must show tremendous exertion. The audience has to feel the strain, stress and effort of the dancers because all these movements convey a message to the viewer. In other words, the modern dancer and choreographer are not afraid to let the audience participate, albeit visually, in the dance.

The second reason involves the flexibility of the body. It would indeed be unfair to describe a ballet dancer's body as inflexible, but we must remember that her body has to respect the rules of classical ballet. Some movements are acceptable, while others are not, because they have no meaning in the language of ballet. The modern dancer, being less restricted by tradition, has greater freedom in the range of body movement. Stretching is one of the most important ways of developing the flexibility required for these movements.

Despite the criticism by modern dancers, ballet is not a static art form, and throughout the years has incorporated changes within its classical framework. Today ballet dancers are required to do exercises that would bring tears of frustration to Marie Taglioni's eyes. In her day, for example, the extended leg in an arabesque formed a 90-degree angle with the body. Now most intermediate students can raise their leg well above waist level. They have been taught that a ballerina must have a beautiful extension. The higher the leg, the more beautiful the pose.

As a result, ballet instruction has developed exercises that train the dancers to perform these "new" steps. Some of the exercises, especially the stretches, have come from modern dance. Since these exercises are relatively new to traditional ballet, they have not been universally adopted. Some teachers enthusiastically accept them, while others energetically reject them. Many suggest a wise blending of certain exercises for certain bodies.

Despite the disagreement over stretching exercises, there are a few "classics" which have become almost legitimate members of the ballet family. At the end of barre practice, many teachers have students do various stretches with one leg on the barre. For example, a student faces the barre and raises one leg to the second position and places it on the barre. Then she slowly shifts the axis of the body away from the supporting leg toward the extended one. As the extended leg slides along the barre, the erect position of the back must be maintained, despite the shift of weight. When the dancer can slide no farther, she should slowly begin to pull her body back toward the supporting leg. If done properly, this exercise stretches the muscles in the inner thigh and improves the extension. It is customary to do a penché (bend with the body) to both sides in order to stretch the waist muscles. The dancer may also shift the axis of the body away from the extended leg. In this case, the extended leg slides along the barre, but follows the movement of the body. These exercises should be repeated to both sides.

This stretch may also be done with the leg on the barre in the croisée or ouverte position to the front. The dancer should raise the free arm above the head and slowly bend the entire torso toward the extended leg, while keeping the spine as straight as possible. Many times, the dancer holds on to the ankle of the extended leg and pulls her body down till her forehead touches the instep. The torso is then raised slowly to the erect position, and bent backward. This exercise is particularly important for girls because it builds up extension and flexibility for adagio. Sometimes the extended leg is slid slowly along the barre and then returned to the original position before the penché to the front and back.

This exercise may be done with the leg in arabesque on the barre (first or fourth arabesque); the extended leg may be slid along the barre, if desired. Usually the dancer bends first to the back and then, for the penché forward, raises the extended leg as high as possible—hoping to form a complete split. This movement is, of course, fundamental for perfecting the arabesque penchée.

Jambe à la main

Though this particular stretch can be done by all dancers, it is specifically geared for girls since it improves extension and flexibility in the waist. The beneficial effects are lost if this exercise is done without regard for correct body alignment. The dancer must be careful not to do quick, jerky penchés because they would increase the risk of straining a muscle.

Another "classic" for improving extension is the famous jambe (pied) à la main, almost universally reserved for women. Here the dancer stands in fifth position with one hand on the barre. She slowly raises her leg into a passé, takes the heel (beginners should take the ankle) in the free hand, and extends the leg to the front as she does a plié. Naturally, the turnout and the correct body placement must be respected. Then, ever so slowly, she moves her leg to the second as she straightens the bent knee, and pulls the heel as high as possible. Finally she releases the heel without lowering her leg. This exercise requires flexibility, but above all, tremendous muscle control.

The corresponding stretch to the back is slightly different. In one version, the dancer raises her back leg into an attitude (a pose with the back leg raised and bent at the knee at a 90-degree angle), places her free hand under the bent knee of the raised leg and pulls her leg into as high an attitude as possible. She may or may not bend forward as she pulls her leg higher. Sometimes she extends the leg into an arabesque, and then lets go without lowering the leg.

In another version, she stands in sixth position with one hand on the barre. She raises her leg in a turned-in passé until the heel is resting under the buttock. Then she grabs the toe of her raised leg with the free hand and pulls her leg as high as she can. Together the arm and leg form a circle. In this exercise, the turnout is forgotten because the dancer concentrates on increasing the flexibility of the back muscles. Greater flexibility improves the sinuous, willowy bends required for adagio movements.

To my knowledge, nobody has calculated the amount of time a dancer spends on the floor—sometimes resting, but usually stretching. On the basis of my personal experience, I would judge the average time to be rather high. After the exercises on the barre, many dancers lie down on the floor and perform a variety of stretches. One of the most common is the split (or grand écart, an acrobatic movement), either to the front with the legs in fourth, or to the side with the legs in second. In both versions, however, the turnout must be rigidly respected. Splits to the side are more difficult. Usually this exercise is reserved for women, though some male dancers practice it to improve their extension.

Another common stretch on the floor involves pulling the turned-in knee up to the chin with jerky little "bounces." This exercise limbers the muscles at the back of the thighs. Teena practices daily an extremely difficult but effective stretch for improving her extension. Actually it is a variation of the jambe à la main, done on the floor. Lying on her back with the head slightly raised, she lifts her right leg to the front as high as possible. Then she takes the heel in her left hand and pulls it to the second until her extended leg is flat on the floor next to her right shoulder. Finally she lowers her head so that her neck is

Stretching in arabesque

Stretch to the back

resting on her left arm and her spine is completely flat on the floor. It is important, she insists, to use the opposite hand, otherwise the body will tilt too much toward the raised leg, and the beneficial effects of this stretch will be lost.

Teena also does a floor variation of the leg stretch to the back with the leg in a turned-in attitude. First she does a complete split to the fourth, and bends her back knee. She grabs the right toe with the right hand, and pulls until she can literally "kiss" her toe! If these exercises sound impossible . . . they just about are. Only the few can survive such contortions.

Needless to say, all these stretches require tremendous muscle flexibility, and should never be done by beginning students. Incorrect or sloppy stretching, even by strong dancers, can cause minor strains and pains, sometimes even serious injuries. All the above exercises should be done *only* after the muscles have been correctly warmed up, never before.

There are, of course, other stretches (usually on the floor) which incorporate the characteristic bounces or the "contract and release" technique of modern dance. The choice of these exercises usually reflects the personal preferences or needs of the individual dancer. Some dancers practice a whole series of pre-barre warm-up exercises on the floor. In their opinion, these floor exercises are helpful because they allow them to concentrate on correct body placement without having to worry about balance. When the dancer is ex-

The splits

Jambe à la main on the floor

Variation on the splits

tended on the floor, her weight is evenly distributed; therefore, she can work specifically on strengthening those muscles required for correct body alignment. An interesting theory, but one that has not met with universal acceptance.

*   *   *

An injury means pain for anybody, but when a dancer is injured, the pure physical pain is compounded with psychological pain. The usual cure is not dancing, but that is bitter medicine for any dancer.

In order to make the "return to normal" less painful, many dancers seek the help of specialists to rehabilitate injured muscles. Carola Trier's studio on West Fifty-eighth Street in New York City is always packed with dancers, who limp in complaining about bad pain, and limp out complaining about good pain. Though I firmly contend that pain is pain, Teena is amazed at my short memory. "After all," she insists, with a note of sarcasm in her voice, "you used to dance. Was it so long ago that you've forgotten?" So I agree with her pain theories, and quickly change the subject.

Carola's studio is a mecca for many dancers. On her strange contraptions equipped with evil-looking springs and Junglegym bars, you will see people (not all of whom are dancers) stretching, pulling, swinging and pushing. You will not have the vaguest idea of what they are doing. But Carola does, as she nimbly hops from bars to springs, and keeps an eye on what everyone is doing. She teaches "muscle controlology," a system of exercises that she learned from Joseph Pilates after a serious injury. Without Pilates's help, Carola swears, she would have been an invalid.

Muscle controlology develops the muscles in such a way that the body eventually performs at full capacity. Most of the exercises involve working with or against springs—a method that incorporates the "contract and release" principle of modern dance. The dancer must learn the fundamental exercises, and then coordinate them with correct posture and proper breathing.

Coordination is the key to Carola's routine. "After all," she says, smiling, "the body is useless if it doesn't function as a unit." And she really has a point. Even for those of us who are not special people like the dancers, what good is a foot without a leg and a leg without a body?

Chapter 5

On Your Toes:
For Girls Only!

Some of my most vivid childhood memories center around long, often tearful scenes involving the respective rights of sisters. I, being the older, felt entitled to be part of the adult world and enjoy its privileges. I also felt entitled to relegate Teena, my younger sister, to the world of children. As far as I was concerned, Teena would just have to wait her turn until she too could join the "big" people. The only trouble was that Teena did not share my firm conviction. Actually she did not care which world she belonged to, as long as she could do exactly what I did. When I started wearing pale, almost invisible lipstick, Teena wanted her own. "But, Mother," I whined, "she's too little. I wasn't allowed to wear lipstick at *her* age." Or the straight, tight skirts that I considered the symbol of womanhood. When Mother actually bought Teena her own straight, tight skirt, I protested bitterly against such injustice. But somehow or other, Mother always soothed my ruffled feelings, and convinced me that generosity toward Teena's whims, not the lipstick or the straight skirt, was the real sign of being a "big" person.

Mother succeeded in maintaining this delicate equilibrium until I started taking ballet lessons. At first everything seemed to go along smoothly. Teena took ballet classes at the same school, wore a black leotard like mine and pinned her hair into a ballet bun. The idyll ended abruptly when I came home one afternoon and proudly announced that I could start toe dancing. The teacher had decided that my class—not Teena's, I added with a tiny grin of triumph—was ready to begin. I was delirious with delight as my dream

The Dying Swan

seemed to be coming true. I would finally own a beautiful pair of pink satin toe slippers and spin on my toes like all the ballerinas I had seen on stage. And best of all, Teena would watch me with envy. I had finally won my rights.

As is often the case, there was some truth in my childish fantasy, but there was also a portion of harsh reality that I had innocently overlooked. Indeed, Teena, despite mournful pleas for Mother to do something about the situation, was not allowed to begin toe dancing because the teacher insisted that her muscles were still too weak. The day I was fitted for my new toe slippers, Teena just had to sit by and watch.

My triumph was short-lived. I had not anticipated how much the pretty pink shoes would hurt my poor toes. As I clumsily hobbled through those first ten minutes, I was close to tears because of the pain. When I looked in the mirror, I did not see that beautiful ballerina of my dreams. Had it not been for my pride and Teena's envy, I would probably have thrown away those pink instruments of torture. At that moment, I desperately longed to be a child, like Teena.

*　　*　　*

I was certainly not the first, nor the last, aspiring little ballerina to be disillusioned by the physical pain of toe dancing. On stage the ballerina seems so beautiful that the audience forgets she is really a person, not a nymph or an enchanted swan. Surprisingly enough, however, toe dancing is a relatively recent invention. When Mlle Lafontaine, the first professional female dancer, appeared in the Paris Opera production of *Le Triomphe de l'Amour* in 1691, she did not look like the typical ballerina of today. She wore a long, heavy costume, an imposing headdress and high-heeled slippers, which confined her dancing to elaborate gliding steps and elegant poses.

Since the male dancers in the seventeenth and eighteenth centuries were less encumbered by heavy costumes, they excelled in complicated leaps (the so-called entrechats) and turns (pirouettes). When Marie Camargo, the famous French ballerina, shortened her skirt a few inches above the instep, so that she could perform jumps and quick allegro steps with greater freedom, she caused a scandal. As a safety precaution, she wore a kind of pantaloon, the *caleçon*

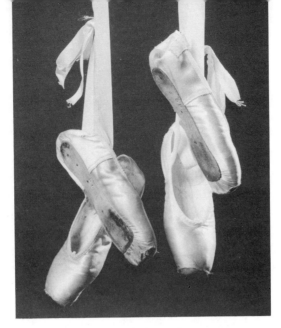

Broken-in toe shoes ready for performance

de précaution—a forerunner of modern ballet tights—to avoid embarrassing situations.[1] Camargo also wore slippers without heels. Those revolutionary new shoes enabled her to jump higher and to point her toes, an innovation that paved the way for the development of toe slippers.

Dancing on toe—in ballet jargon, on pointe—was not really "born" until the beginning of the nineteenth century. It is difficult to pinpoint the exact date because there are only a few vague references to dancers on toe and an 1821 lithograph showing a ballerina prettily posed on pointe. It was the great Marie Taglioni who made toe dancing famous. In the 1832 production of *La Sylphide,* choreographed by her father, she immortalized the Romantic ballet dancer in her frothy white ankle-length skirt and her pointe shoes.

Because the early toe shoes were soft slippers darned on the sides and under—though not directly under—the toes, the ballerina could only pose gracefully on both pointes and do a few arabesques. Still, the introduction of pointe work was considered revolutionary because it elongated the dancer's movements and epitomized the dreamy qualities of the Romantic ballerina.[2]

When Taglioni went to Russia, in 1837, she electrified her audiences. After one performance, some of her fans bought a pair of her used slippers for two hundred rubles, and made "toe shoe" broth—using Taglioni's shoes in place of the more conventional chicken—which they all ceremoniously sipped at an elegant banquet in honor of the great star. Such was the fame of Taglioni's pointe shoes!

Toward 1862, toe slippers were "blocked"—that is, the tips of the toes were stiffened with glue and then darned for greater support. Now the ballerina was able to perform more complex steps, such as long, suspended adagio movements with her partner, various types of pirouettes and relevés on one foot. The Italian ballerinas who danced Petipa's ballets before the czar and his court at the Maryinsky Theater were acclaimed for the brilliant technique they had learned at the Academy of Dance at La Scala. One in particular, Pierina Legnani (1863–1923), made ballet history in 1895 when she introduced thirty-two fouettés into the Black Swan pas de deux.[3] The Russian audiences applauded her virtuosity, while her rival, the Russian ballerina Mathilde Kschessinska, watched jealously from the wings. When Kschessinska later executed thirty-two perfect fouettés, the crowds went wild because a Russian ballerina had finally reached the level of the foreign stars. Legnani and Kschessinska were the only ballerinas in the history of the Maryinsky Theater to receive the title of *prima ballerina assoluta,* the greatest homage the czar could offer a dancer.

*   *   *

Modern pointe shoes are still made by hand. Contrary to popular legend, they contain no steel, wood or concrete. They are usually made of soft leather covered with pink, though sometimes black or white, satin, with a drawstring which the dancer adjusts so that the shoes will not buckle. After she has pulled the two ends of the drawstring to the desired tightness, she ties two or three knots and snips the strings. This is an important professional touch for two reasons. First of all, a dancer can trip if the strings are not cut; secondly, it is not attractive to see long strings hanging over the ballerina's toes.

The hard toe of the shoe, the so-called box, is made from seven layers of cloth that have been stiffened with special glue. Professional dancers usually special-order their shoes, specifying the requirements best suited to their feet. The vamp, or front part of the box, can be made longer if the dancer has a high instep; this will keep her already too flexible foot from rolling over on her toes too much. The vamp can be made shorter if the dancer has a low instep; a low vamp will enable her to roll over more, thereby creating the illusion of a high instep. Some dancers prefer a square, flat tip on the boxes of their shoes; others a more rounded, narrow one.

The sole of the pointe slipper is made of leather on the outside, with a special inner sole of strong leather called the shank. This reinforced inner sole gives the foot additional support, but some dancers prefer a three-quarter or half shank.

It is the dancer's responsibility to sew on the ribbons and elastics. The correct place for attaching the ribbons is found by pressing down the backs of the shoe. The ribbons are sewn where the sides bend. It is imperative that the ribbons be sewn securely because a loose ribbon can cause the dancer to trip or even fall. Most dancers also add a three-quarter-inch strip of elastic, which goes around the instep for greater support and insurance against loose ribbons.

The correct method of tying ribbons is to crisscross them over the instep, wind them once around the ankle and then knot them firmly in the back. The ribbons should be secure enough not to bag, but loose enough not to stop the circulation. Since the ribbons usually loosen up a bit during dancing, the ballerina learns to calculate just how tight she must tie them. The ends of the ribbons must be tucked neatly under the ribbons. Teena soon learned that one of the arch sins for professional ballet dancers is loose ribbon ends on stage. After one of her first performances with the New York City Ballet company, the ballet mistress stormed angrily into the dressing room and loudly criticized Teena's lack of professionalism, right in front of all the other dancers. Upon seeing Teena practically reduced to tears, one of the older girls told her that the only way to avoid this problem was to wet her ribbon ends, to glue them or to sew them. Even today one of the last things Teena does before going on stage is to check her ribbons.

Since toe shoes are made by hand, they are very expensive. Stock shoes average about eighteen dollars a pair, special orders several dollars more. Ballet students have to buy their own, while most professional dancers receive free, though not unlimited, shoes from their company. Since toe shoes do not last indefinitely, keeping a dancer supplied is a costly affair for parents and ballet companies alike. The life of a pair of toe shoes depends upon the use—or more correctly, the abuse—it receives. For students who take one to

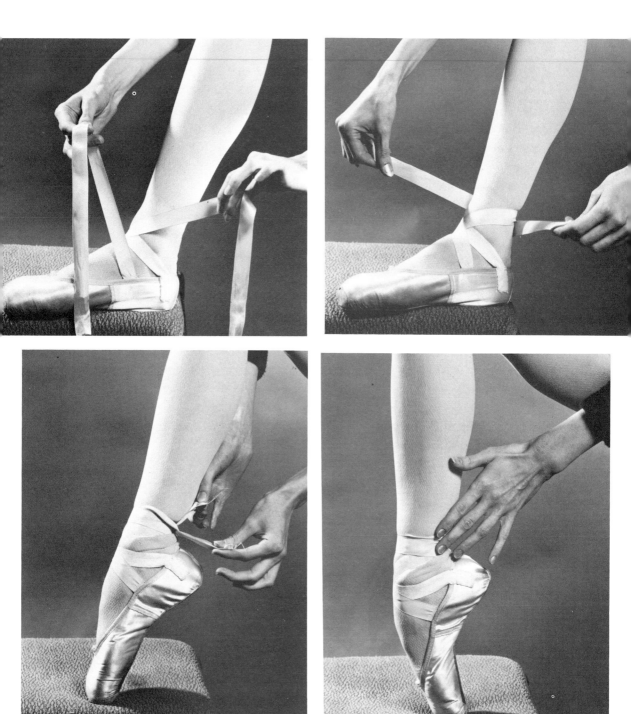

Tying a toe shoe

two pointe classes per week, the shoes will last a month or so, but even here there are individual variations. Some girls wear out their shoes quickly, and have difficulty dancing on soft shoes; others get much longer wear from their shoes. Generally speaking, the stronger the dancer, the longer she can wear her shoes.

For performance, a dancer does not always use new shoes. In lyrical, less technical ballets like *La Valse* or *Serenade*, Teena chooses old, soft shoes because they permit greater ease of movement. In ballets with lots of jumps, she usually prefers soft shoes because they do not "clunk." Nothing breaks the spell of ballet like the *thump thump* of hard slippers. In highly demanding, more technical ballets like *Concerto Barocco* or *Symphony in C*, Teena wears hard shoes. All those exacting steps on pointe would "kill" her feet, she explains with a frown of simulated pain.

Nothing is more erroneous than thinking that ballerinas tie on their new pointe shoes, fasten up their costumes and race out on stage to perform *Giselle* or *Swan Lake*. Toe shoes must be "broken in" before they are worn on stage. The tips of the shoes are usually beaten vigorously against the floor. It may seem disrespectful to the toe slippers, but this technique helps take out the "clunk." Teena usually cuts away the satin from the tip of her shoes to reduce the chances of slipping. She maintains that it is better and safer this way, and the tip will be worn away anyhow.

The next step in the breaking-in routine is practicing little exercises like relevé, échappé or passé—the big ones are too dangerous with new shoes. The heat from the dancer's feet begins to mold the shoes and soften the glue in the box. As the shoes take on the shape of the dancer's feet, she begins to perform more complicated steps. But not too many, or else her shoes will be too soft for performance.

If Teena is running low on toe shoes, as can happen on long tours, she has her own "home-style" method of hardening shoes. She pours about a tablespoonful of Fabulon, a commercial varnish, into the boxes, rotates the shoes so the varnish will be evenly distributed, and repeats this process until she feels that the boxes have absorbed enough varnish. Then she lets the shoes dry for about twenty-four hours, before using them again on stage and in class. I asked Teena if she can feel a difference between the regular toe shoes and the "Fabuloned" ones. She admits that the "Fabuloned" ones may hurt the toes more, especially if the skin is sensitive to the combination of Fabulon, nylon tights and perspiration. "But for *my* hoofs," she adds laughingly, " 'Fabuloned' shoes are great!"

＊　＊　＊

Good ballet training is always desirable, but it is essential for pointe work because the student would otherwise be unaware of the hidden dangers. And by hidden dangers, I mean more than broken toes or sprained ankles. Far too often, ballet teachers, sometimes under pressure from overambitious mothers, permit students to start pointe work before they are technically prepared, and worse still, before they are old enough. Here lies the real danger. Toe dancing at too early an age with insufficient or improper training can cause thick, muscular legs, deformed toes and even more serious problems. Many times, friends are amazed when they learn that I used to dance professionally. "But you have such nice legs," they object. "You couldn't possibly have toe-danced." I was fortunate to go to a school where we were permitted to begin toe only after two to three years of serious basic training, *if* we were older than ten and *if* the teacher felt we were strong enough. Many little girls were upset, and many mothers offended, but Fred Danieli was firm. He knew what he was doing.

Before we even stood on toe, we learned about the various positions of the feet. The foot could be flat—that is, firmly planted on the ground. This is the basic starting position for most ballet movements. We could use the foot in demi-pointe—half toe to many American ballet students. In ballet, there are two types of demi-pointe: the low demi-pointe, where the heel is barely raised off the ground, and the high demi-pointe, where the weight rests on the ball of the foot. While the low demi-pointe is rarely used, the high demi-pointe is of primary importance, especially for men, who do not go on toe. Finally, there is the full pointe, where the dancer stands on her toes. Today there are two possibilities: the classical pointe position, where the weight is on the tips of the toes, and the neoclassical position, where the dancer overarches and actually stands on buckled toes. In the Romantic era, the ballerinas rose obliquely on pointe because the only support in the shoes came from the darning under the toes. With the invention of blocked toes, the ballerina was able to rise vertically on pointe into the classical position.

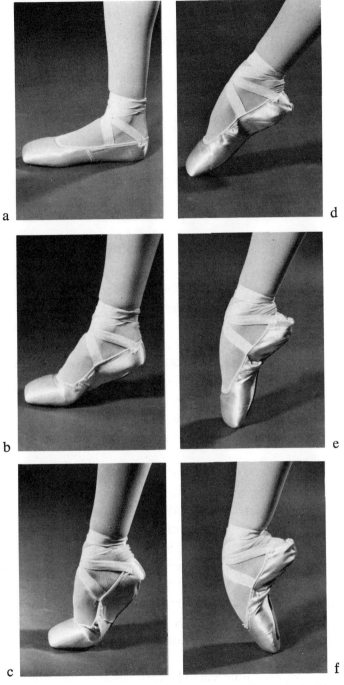

Positions of the feet in ballet: (a) flat on the ground; (b) low demi-pointe; (c) high demi-pointe; (d) oblique (Romantic period position); (e) full pointe (Classical position); (f) full pointe (Neoclassical position).

After the explanation of the foot positions, we began to do some pointe work during the last ten minutes of the regular ballet class. Initially, we worked with two hands on the barre and did simple pliés and relevés on two feet in first, second, fourth and fifth positions. After a few sous-sus (a relevé in fifth position traveling in any direction with the feet tightly closed), we attempted a few échappés, and had the usual beginners' difficulty in coordinating the movement of both legs as they shot out from fifth position to second and then back into fifth with a plié. Our ankles wobbled and our toes throbbed, but we were all too proud to admit defeat.

Then we attempted the same exercises with only one hand on the barre. This was more difficult since we had to readjust the body equilibrium that we had learned for demi-pointe work. For ballet in general, but particularly for toe, body placement is the key factor and muscle control the second. Mr. Danieli told us to "pull up"—that is, draw all our weight off those poor burning toes and use the buttocks, back and stomach muscles. Doing these same simple steps off barre with no support except our muscles was a real challenge, because we often missed the correct body placement, especially if the tempo was brisk. And then we stumbled, and sometimes fell.

As time passed, the exercises seemed easier because our muscles were stronger and our feet were tougher. Though it may sound unromantic, dancers have tough ugly feet. Years of toe dancing produce thick, discolored toenails (toenails have to be cut short and blunt; otherwise they will act like knives), gnarled joints that are perfect sites for blisters, and ugly soft corns. No dancer, to my knowledge, has ever been hired to model sandals!

A dancer must take good care of her precious feet, since they are the single most important instrument for her work. She covers the bad toes with Band-Aids and usually wraps a bit of lamb's wool or paper towel (facial tissues and toilet paper are soft, but disintegrate too easily) around the tips of the toes to act as padding against the rubbing of the hard box. Sometimes professional dancers are not able to perform because of sore feet—infected soft corns, inflamed bunions, or bone spurs that sometimes have to be removed by an operation.

As soon as the girls are strong enough, they begin pointe classes once or twice a week. These classes are indeed for girls only, and concentrate on developing the techniques of pointe work. They follow the same basic pattern as the regular ballet classes, with approximately half the time spent on the barre and the other half in the center of the room. Even the exercises on the barre followed the basic routine of any ballet class—from the warm-up pliés to the tendus to the jetés and the battements—but the teacher emphasizes how these basic steps are important for pointe work. Much time is spent on body placement, which is especially important for pirouettes and adagio work with a partner. There are also many exercises involving extension—the dancer's ability to raise her leg as high as possible while respecting the rigid laws of body placement. Extension is more challenging on pointe. All ballerinas strive for the highest arabesque possible, and spend many hours before the mirrors perfecting the spectacular arabesque penchée (an arabesque with the torso tipped so the leg can reach greater height), with the legs in a complete split.

The various kinds of pirouettes that the girl learned to do on demi-pointe have then to be performed on pointe. She has to do a relevé on pointe, which involves lifting all her weight to the toes of one foot, before she begins to turn. This relevé requires greater strength in the legs, but especially in the back, buttocks and abdominal muscles, and greater precision in finding the exact balance. The landing from a pirouette on pointe is tricky because the girl must be careful to have both feet come down softly and simultaneously into a demi-plié. Beginners tend to land first with the supporting foot and then the other; the effect created by this clumsy landing is noisy and unattractive.

On stage the ballerina performs both unsupported and supported pirouettes, but in class she must be able to do all types of pirouettes by herself. In theory, a partner only enables the ballerina to do more turns than she could by herself—with a partner she could do up to ten pirouettes, while alone she can do four, or in the case of an exceptionally strong dancer, five turns—and to end in spectacular positions. For example, it would be physically impossible, without a partner's support, to land in an arabesque penchée after a triple pirouette. In practice, however, a good partner assists the ballerina in regaining her balance whenever she begins to fall off pointe.

One of the best-known ballet steps is the pas de bourrée couru, usually shortened to bourrée. This is a series of small, quick running steps, usually done on pointe. When it is performed correctly, the ballerina seems to float across the stage. Her feet should resemble a precision drill with their rapid, even and seemingly effortless movement. The bourrée can also be performed while the ballerina stands in one place. This step coupled with proper arm

Révérence

movements can convey a wide array of emotion—the fear of the Swan Queen Odette when she first meets Prince Siegfried and begs him not to shoot her swan companions, or the haunting melancholy of the sleepwalker in Balanchine's *La Sonnambula.* The bourrée has been immortalized in *The Dying Swan,* the short ballet which Fokine choreographed for Anna Pavlova in 1905. The entire ballet consists of a series of intricate bourrées. Pavlova's quivering bourrées and rippling arms, which seemed transformed into wings, described more than the Swan's agonizing death; they expressed the universal tragedy of death for all living creatures.

Dancers perform these deceptively effortless bourrées only after years of constant practice. The steps in a correct bourrée should be neither too slow nor too big; one foot must never drag behind the other. The rhythmic beating of the feet must be even, while the upper body and arms seem to float. Bourrée is difficult and tiring, and worst of all hurts those poor toes, as all dancers know.

When a dancer has reached the semi-professional or professional level, she usually wears pointe shoes to every ballet class. More often than not, they are old, soft shoes which permit her to work easily on demi-pointe, though she may do some of the barre exercises on full pointe to strengthen her feet. Other times, she may do the barre exercises in new shoes to break them in. Wearing pointe shoes becomes a question of habit, because after years of dancing on toe, the soft ballet slippers seem strange. Teena does not even own a pair of ordinary ballet slippers. If she needs a pair, she simply "deshanks"—that is, rips out the strong leather inner sole—a pair of old toe shoes. Most professional dancers prefer to work on pointe as often as possible because too many relevés on demi-pointe can build up strong, knotty calf muscles.

*   *   *

As the pointe class draws to an end the dancers show signs of fatigue. They mop their perspiring brows more frequently, bend over to catch their breath, and shake their tired legs to loosen up the muscles that have started to cramp from strain. A few girls even remove their shoes, massage their aching toes and then put the shoes back on. But every girl in the class, no matter how tired or discouraged she may feel, stands neatly in place and draws herself up regally for the final révérence, or curtsy, to the teacher. All the dancers, from the little country girl just beginning her professional training to the great star, bow respectfully to the teacher. After all, ballet was born in the royal courts of Europe, and the traditions of courtly etiquette still hold, even in our modern, democratically informal world.

Chapter 6

Off Barre: The Beginning of the Challenge

Stepping into the center of the practice studio is perhaps the most important moment in class. Here the real challenge begins. The steps on the barre are strenuous and tiring. Above all, they are aimed at training specific muscles, improving balance and perfecting body placement. During the barre, the dancer concentrates on technical specifics and does not think about dancing. It is impossible to dance on barre.

Off barre, the dancer has to apply the fundamentals learned on barre. Balance and correct body placement are key factors because the dancer no longer depends on the extra support of the barre. If her body placement is incorrect, she loses her balance and sometimes falls. Off barre, the dancer no longer works first to one side and then to the other. She has to learn to alternate her feet without any visible sign of strain.

The exercises off barre are challenging because they involve the added element of movement. The dancer is not fixed to the same spot, but performs steps in all directions—to the front (en avant), to either side (à la seconde), to the back (en arrière), on a diagonal (en diagonal) and in a circle (en manège). In other words, she must learn to take full advantage of the space at her disposal.

The steps off barre belong to two basic categories. They can be terre à terre (on the ground) or ballonné (bouncing like a ball). Historically speak-

Variation of saut de chat

ing, the terre à terre steps are the older. Ballet developed from court dances, which were based on complex patterns formed by groups of dancers. The direction of the movement in the dances was horizontal. Later on, however, vertical steps were introduced. They were more spectacular, easier for the audience to see on a raised stage, and more competitive. The vertical or air-oriented style (which Carlo Blasis named the ballon) suited the artistic and ideological exigencies of Romantic ballet, where the emphasis was on other-worldliness. The sylphlike ballerina raised herself on pointe, leaped through the mists and floated up toward the heavens.

Perhaps the most difficult aspect of the off barre movements is the transition from one step to another. Transitions should appear effortless, and should never detract from the important steps that follow. Easier said than done, because many of these transitions involve rapid shifts of direction. For example, after a series of rapid turns on the diagonal to the right, the dancer may be required to start the same sequence to the left at the same speed. Unless she has full control, she will not be able to move easily and gracefully into the turns to the left.

The real challenge of the off barre exercises is dancing. This does not mean that technique, body placement and respect for classical ballet rules can be forgotten. On the contrary, all these technical elements must be combined into a harmonious flow of controlled movements. But to this harmonious flow the student must add a touch of herself, a part of her soul, so to speak, which transforms these technical movements into something expressive. Unless there are feeling and expression behind the technique, there is no real dancing. It is this special touch of "soul," rather than technical skill, that separates the classroom dancer from the real dancer.

As soon as the student steps into the center of the practice studio, she must pretend that she is on stage. Instead of mirrors, she should imagine the audience. Although a dancer may pretend that she is dancing for tens of thousands of applauding fans, she cannot resist the only too human temptation to watch—sometimes admire, sometimes criticize—herself in the mirrors. While self-observation can be a helpful method for correcting poor positions or ungraceful lines, it can, and usually does, become a bad habit. Teena will never forget her first performance on the big New York stage. "I was nervous just at the thought of being out in front of all those people," she recalls.

"When the curtain went up, I felt completely disoriented. Instead of the friendly mirrors, I saw a huge black mass, filled with eyes that I couldn't see but that could see me. It was terrifying! But once you're out on stage, you have to dance."

All dancers feel this strange sense of emptiness when they stare into the black audience pit. The strong spotlights and footlights are so bright that all newcomers feel dizzy. But after a while, they get used to the new dimension of dancing on stage.

In order to stop students from using the mirror as a crutch, some teachers have the class turn their backs to it and then do various combinations. Many students immediately feel uncomfortable.

Although there are no fixed dimensions for a practice studio, ideally it should approximate the size of the average stage. In the New York State Theater, the large practice studio is identical in size to the stage. In this way, rehearsals can be held in either place, and the dancers do not have to worry about changing their spacing.

The floor of the studio is wood,[1] which must *never* be waxed. In order to prevent slides and falls, the dancer often rubs rosin on the toes and heels of her shoes. In the nineteenth century, the antidote for slipping was simply wetting the floor with a watering can! But water dries quickly, and today the picturesque watering can has generally been replaced by the rosin box that every ballet studio has hidden in one corner. In emergencies, however, wetting the floor or even sprinkling it with Comet or a comparable cleaning powder is better than slipping.

While Comet theoretically reduces the dancer's risk of slipping, it can produce unexpected side effects. Quite a few years ago, Teena participated in a talent show given by students in the Casa Italiana at Columbia University. She had been scheduled to dance the *Nutcracker* pas de deux at the beginning of the second part. This meant that during intermission she and her partner could run through the adagio and prepare the stage—two and a half cans of Comet all over the beautifully waxed floor. Their performance went well, and raised enthusiastic applause from the audience as well as clouds of green dust from the floor. Nobody really noticed the puffs of Comet until the tenor and soprano (both professionals from the Met) stepped out on stage—and began coughing and choking from the insidious green dust. Afterward, at the reception, the pianist complained that the piano keys were gritty and green. But that's show business. *Pazienza,* as the Italians say, with a slight shrug of their shoulders.

*   *   *

Theoretically the exercises off barre parallel those on barre. Since the off-barre exercises require more space, the dancers form two smaller groups. This division also allows them to rest between the combinations.

The beginning combinations in the center usually involve terre à terre steps such as battement tendu in various directions with coordinated arm and head movements, rond de jambe à terre, frappé, battement sur le cou-de-pied, and so forth. In these exercises, the student has to concentrate on coordination of the entire body—legs, arms, torso and head—while respecting the rules of body placement.

An important traveling terre à terre step is the glissade, or glide. In the glissade, first the working foot moves from fifth position in the desired direction, and then the supporting foot closes the movement. The glissade is important as a transition step, and tests the student's ability to change direction.

Most of the time off barre, however, is devoted to three general categories of steps: adagio, tours (turns) and sauts (jumps). For the adagio work in the center, the student performs sequences similar to those on the barre. Since the center adagio requires greater balance and muscle control, it builds up the dancer's strength and stamina. Though the girls often rise on pointe for some of the poses, they cannot perform entire sequences, like the grand rond de jambe en l'air, on pointe without support from a partner. In addition to muscular control, the adagio requires great concentration. The dancer has to be especially careful to phrase her movements to match those of the music, since anticipation or lateness is more noticeable in the adagio than in allegro. The adagio is always done in the early part of the center work, when the dancer's muscles are properly warmed up but not tired from the strain of the big jumps.

The girl must concentrate on improving her extension, especially in the développé to the second and the infinite varieties of arabesques and attitudes. A good extension must be well above waist level, with the toe neatly pointed and the knee locked. In order to gain the optical illusion of greater height, some girls will cheat and bend their foot (the toe still pointed) upward at the ankle. The leg indeed looks higher, because the foot is higher, but the angle formed by the turned-up foot breaks the harmonious line of the classical arabesque. Another trick to "steal" extra height in an arabesque is to move the leg, ever so slightly, to the side. It is easier to raise the leg higher in this incorrect position, but from some angles this cheating arabesque is ugly. In both cases height is gained, but the beauty of pure classical lines is compromised.

Another special feature of the adagio is the tour en promenade, a slow, rotating turn on one foot, either by means of little shifts of the heel—if the tour en promenade is done with the foot flat on the ground—or with support from the partner, who moves the girl around on pointe. The tour en promenade can be done with the leg extended in fourth position to the front, to the second, in passé, in arabesque, in attitude or in any combination of these poses. The leg is usually held high.

Along with extension, the dancer must pay careful attention to épaulement (shouldering) in the adagio. This term refers to the special "shouldered" positions in which the torso is twisted to positions halfway between the front (or back) and the side; the head inclines toward the forward shoulder. The épaulement can be croisé (crossed) or effacé (shaded). For the croisé, the right leg is "crossed" in front of the left leg to fourth position, the shoulders form a right angle with the feet and the head leans to the front (right) shoulder. For the effacé, the right leg is opened to fourth position, but the body and the shoulders are placed obliquely to the audience so that part of the body is shaded. Here again the head turns toward the front (left) shoulder. Both the croisé and the effacé positions may be done with either foot, and to the front or back.

Today épaulement constitutes an important part of classical ballet. It adds an artistic touch, and finishes the pose. Épaulement is a relatively recent invention, however, and was rarely used in the old French school.

*　*　*

Tours, or turns, are the second important category of steps done off barre. Some form of turning can be found in all kinds of dance. The simplest, of course, is the turn on two feet, because it requires minimum coordination of

Croisé to fourth position front   *Croisé to fourth position back*

Effacé to fourth position front   *Effacé to fourth position back*

the arms, legs and body. Only the more sophisticated dance forms make use of the turn on one foot, which involves greater muscle control and balance.

In classical ballet, the dancer may do a turn on two feet, on one foot or jumping. In ballet, turns are done on demi-pointe by the men and beginning girls, and on pointe by the girls. Occasionally turns are performed on the flat foot or even on the heel, but only in character-inspired dances.

One of the basic dangers in turns is dizziness. The only solution is "spotting." The dancer must choose a fixed point in the distance (for example, the fire exit sign), then keep her eyes on it as long as she can, even though her body is already following the momentum of the turn. When she can no longer keep her head in that position, she must snap it around quickly and look again at the chosen point. Unless a dancer spots, she will become dizzy and "travel" all over the stage or the classroom. Spotting is difficult. In the classroom, the dancer tends to spot in the mirror; as a result, she often has difficulty turning on the stage, where there are no mirrors. She must train herself to spot on stage.

Spotting is particularly difficult for the near-sighted. While they may succeed in spotting on some large, obvious object in class, they are virtually "blind" on stage, because the lighting varies from ballet to ballet. Thus they cannot depend on a guaranteed object for spotting.

Near-sighted dancers can solve the problem with contact lenses. But the benefits of perfect vision are not immediate, as Teena and many other dancers have discovered. When I finally convinced Teena to try the new contact lenses, she was already in the company. I was delighted that I had finally broken down her obstinate reluctance to get perfect vision with those miraculous plastic disks. My strongest argument was that her turns, which were her weak point, would improve. Even Teena seemed thoroughly convinced of her decision as we walked to her lens-fitting appointment. On the way back to our apartment, Teena spoke enthusiastically about how she was going to become a "great turner," thanks to her new lenses.

A few days later, Teena stormed into the apartment after three hours of rehearsal and threw her ballet bag into the corner. I paid little attention to her angry muttering, and dismissed her nasty behavior as typical ballet "bitchiness," until she stalked over to me and growled, "Thanks—thanks a lot. Because of you and your stupid advice, I can no longer turn. I cannot even do a single pirouette."

Though I usually have a quick tongue, the vehemence of her accusations left me speechless. It was only later in the evening that I understood what the trouble was. Since Teena had learned to turn with poor vision, she actually fell off balance when she could see perfectly! Fortunately she had the constancy to relearn how to balance and spot with the lenses. Now she cannot dance without them. Strange as it may seem to those who see well, it is difficult to dance with perfect vision if one has learned with imperfect vision!

The two most important turns on two feet are the détourné and the enveloppé. For the détourné, the dancer turns backward on pointe or on demi-pointe in the direction of the back foot. For the enveloppé, the back foot does a rond de jambe en dedans and propels the body around in a turn to the right. The détourné and the enveloppé are opposite, and yet complementary, turns.

The déboulés (also called tours chaînés) are rapidly rotating turns in which the dancer steps quickly from one foot to the other while turning. The legs must be kept close together as she travels across the stage. Since the effect of the déboulés is spectacular, these turns are commonly used at the end of a solo variation. Although déboulés were probably used in the dances of ancient Greece, they were introduced into classical ballet by the Italian school in the late nineteenth century. Pierina Legnani and Virginia Zucchi, both trained at the Academy of Dance at La Scala in Milan, supposedly brought the déboulés to Russia.

Turns on one foot, either on demi-pointe or on pointe, are called pirouettes. A pirouette offers the real test of perfect balance, because the body must remain strong and erect from the preparation, through the turn, to the landing (which is perhaps one of the most difficult moments in the pirouette). The momentum for the turn is gained from the preparation in demi-plié, from the shoulders and the arms, and from the snapping motion of the head in spotting. There are two basic kinds of pirouettes: the tour piqué, in which the dancer steps onto one leg for the turn, and the pirouette relevée, in which the dancer raises her weight onto one foot. The variations on the kind and number of pirouettes are infinite. They can be done in various positions from various preparations; the turn may be outside (en dehors) or inside (en dedans).

In the most common version of the tour piqué, the dancer steps onto one foot (on demi- or full pointe) and turns with the working leg in passé. The turn is usually done in a series, with the dancer moving on the diagonal or in a circle. The bent foot can be placed at the knee if the tour piqué is slow, or on

Landing in fourth position after pirouette en dehors

the calf if the tour piqué is rapid. The turns can be single, multiple or even alternating.

Tour piqué can also be done in attitude or arabesque. Both these versions are slower than the tour piqué in passé. Here the emphasis is on grace and elegance, not speed. Tour piqué in second position is relatively rare because of the difficulty in keeping the leg in second position à la hauteur during the turn. With the momentum from the turn, the extended leg tends to drop or move slightly forward. Both "faults" spoil the harmonious line of the turn.

For the pirouette relevée, the dancer turns on one foot on demi-pointe or on pointe, and holds the working leg in a passé. The turn may start from one or both feet. The most common preparations for the pirouette relevée are (1) pas de bourrée into fourth position with a demi-plié; (2) échappé into fourth position with a demi-plié. The turns may be single or multiple, inside or outside. Good female dancers should do a triple pirouette on pointe. Good male dancers do many more pirouettes on the demi-pointe.

The pirouette relevée may also be done from the fifth position, with a preparation either from a relevé in fifth position or an échappé closing in fifth. Here again the turn may be single or multiple, inside or outside. Very often pirouettes from fifth position are done in a series.

There is considerable discussion about the exact placement of the leg in passé during the pirouette. The position ranges anywhere from the sur le cou-de-pied position to midcalf to the knee, and often depends on the school. George Balanchine, for example, insists that all pirouettes be done with the working leg in a high passé. Sometimes the speed of the pirouette can determine the height of the bent leg.

Common pirouettes relevées that start from one or both feet are the turn in arabesque, the turn in attitude and the challenging turn in second, which is usually reserved for male dancers. Here the dancer does a full turn à la seconde, and continues the turns in succession. The spectacular counterpart for the female is the fouetté, where the whipping circular motion of the working leg creates the momentum for the turns. Fouettés are always done in a series, and are commonly used to end solo variations. Today it is common to have the dancer execute sequences of single, double and occasionally triple fouettés!

In classical ballet, most of the leaping turns are reserved for the men. They require strength, precision and muscular control that are beyond the physical capabilities of the female dancer. This last statement is in no way intended to be derogatory. While the technical virtuosity of the ballerina certainly equals that of the male, she has certain specialties and certain weaknesses that are dictated by her female anatomy. Likewise, the danseur has corresponding specialties and weaknesses that reflect his male anatomy. On the one hand, the ballerina can develop spectacular extension because of the structure of the pelvis. The dramatic effect of the extension is increased by the length of the ballerina's legs. Generally, girls have longer legs, relative to their height, than boys. The man, on the other hand, can jump higher because the muscles of his legs, back and shoulders are innately stronger. This greater muscular strength enables him to perform a wider variety of aerial turns.

Finally, in all fairness to the male dancer, we must remember that ever since the Romantic age of ballet, he has been rudely ignored. For many years he was merely a human crane for the ballerina, who executed exquisite steps on pointe and breathtaking leaps, thanks to his support. The eye-catching jumps that are becoming increasingly popular for the male dancer are, in a certain sense, his belated reaction to generations of forced subservience to the ballerina.

*   *   *

Jumps and leaps can be found in most dance forms in every age. It would appear from prehistoric cave paintings that leaps were used in the cavemen's dance ritual. Even today leaps form an important part of dances among the primitive peoples in Africa and Australia. The leap seems to represent man's attempt to free himself from the bonds of this world and to soar upward. Yet at the same time, this desire to fly symbolizes man's disobedience toward the divinities. Just consider the fate of Icarus, whose marvelous flying wings melted loose when he soared too close to the sun. He fell into the clear blue sea far below, and was thus punished for his transgression.

In classical ballet, the jumps, or sauts, can be divided into several categories. There are the simple movements (temps simples) and the beats (batterie), which can be subdivided into crossed beats (batterie à croisement) and beats with impact (batterie à choc). There are also the turning leaps (which will be discussed in greater detail in the next chapter).

The most simple leap is the sobresaut. Here the dancer starts from a demi-plié (usually in fifth position), pushes off from the floor with both feet and straightens his legs as he jumps forward. He must land in a demi-plié. In classical ballet, the toes must be neatly pointed, the legs tightly straightened and the body held erect. There are, of course, many variations on the sobresaut.

The échappé is a jump in which the feet move ("escape") from an odd-numbered position, usually fifth but occasionally first, to an even-numbered one (second or fourth to the front or back), and then return to the starting position. The dancer begins from a demi-plié in fifth, opens his feet to second (or fourth) as he jumps, lands in that position in a demi-plié, jumps back to fifth and lands in a demi-plié. The échappé may be done with or without a changing of feet—that is, the right foot may start front and close back, or start and end front. The échappé can also be done on pointe. Here the girl slides both feet out briskly to the open position with both legs straight and then returns to fifth. Sometimes, however, she may do a very small jump and land on pointe in the open position. In the échappé, the movement of both legs must be symmetrical. One leg must not open higher or wider than the other; otherwise the effect will be comical.

The assemblé (joining together) is one of the basic leaps in ballet. Here again, the dancer starts from demi-plié in fifth position. As she begins to jump, she straightens one leg directly under her and brings the other to the second position or fourth front or back. At the culmination of the jump, both legs must be extended with the toes pointed: one leg directly under the dancer, and the other to the front, side or back. Both feet must land simultaneously in a demi-plié in fifth position. The assemblé may be done with or without a change of feet. There are many variations on the assemblé.

The sissonne (a step named after its inventor) is really the reversal of the assemblé. Here the dancer starts from demi-plié in fifth position, leaps into the air, kicks out one leg (to the second or to the fourth front or back), and lands on one leg in a demi-plié with the other leg extended in the air. There are an infinite number of variations for the sissonne. Gail Grant lists thirty-eight in her *Technical Manual and Dictionary of Classical Ballet*. The leap can be large (sissonne grande) or small (sissonne petite), done with or without a change of feet, and even double (sissonne doublée), whereby the dancer does a sissonne ouverte to the side, then a coupé, and closes with an assemblé.

For the jeté, the dancer brushes the working foot on the ground as she jumps from one foot to the other. This jump is called jeté because the leg appears to be thrown. Actually the jeté is nothing more than the running step performed according to balletic criteria. When running, we leap onto the front leg as we bend the back one. The same principle is observed for the jeté, but the legs are turned out, the toes pointed and the body held erect.

There are many kinds of jetés—small, large, in all directions. Two famous variations on the jeté are the grand jeté and the saut de chat. The grand jeté is a large, spectacularly athletic leap in which the dancer jumps over an imaginary hurdle with both legs extended in the air—one to the front and the other to the back. The dancer usually starts with a preparatory push-off step, such as a glissade or pas de couru (quick little running steps). Then as she jumps, the right leg is kicked into a high battement to the front. In midair she jumps over the "hurdle" and raises the back leg. At the culminating moment of the leap, both legs are extended in the air. The effect is breathtaking, especially if both legs are opened in a perfect split. She then lands in a demi-plié on the front leg (right) with the back leg (left) in the air in an arabesque or an attitude. In the grand jeté, the dancer must aim at jumping as high as she can and at traveling as far as she can. To gain maximum effect, the grand jeté should always be done in profile, and possibly in a series.

The saut de chat, or cat step, is another eye-catching jump. It is really a jeté in which first one leg and then the other passes through a passé before the landing in demi-plié in fifth position. The dancer should pull the bent knee of both legs as high as she can, so that she appears momentarily suspended. At the culminating moment, both legs are bent in second position in midair.

Recently there has been a tendency to use beats (batterie) in as many jumps as possible. First of all, the inclusion of more beats makes the movements more spectacular. Secondly, complicated beats require greater technical ability, which is becoming increasingly important in today's highly competitive ballet world. Compared to the situation thirty or forty years ago, ballet training has become almost a mass phenomenon. Now there are more, better-trained dancers than ever before. Competition is stiff.

The entrechats are the most common type of batterie à croisement (beaten jumps with crossed feet). In classical ballet, the entrechats are numbered from one to eight. Actually, the term "entrechat un" is never used; it is just a simple jump. Entrechat deux is always called changement. Here the dancer starts in fifth position in a demi-plié with the right foot front. As she jumps into the air with both legs extended under her, she changes her feet, and lands in a demi-plié in fifth position with the left foot front.

There is some controversy as to how the odd-numbered entrechats trois, cinq, sept are done. In the Russian school, the difference between the odd- and even-numbered entrechats is in the landing. The dancer lands on one foot for the odd-numbered entrechats, but on two feet for the even-numbered ones. The number of beats is the same. Thus an entrechat trois is nothing more than a changement battu landing on one foot (if the right foot is front, the entrechat trois ends with the right foot in sur le cou-de-pied derrière), entrechat cinq is really an entrechat quatre landing on one foot (if the right foot is front, the entrechat cinq ends with the left foot in sur le cou-de-pied derrière), and so forth.

In the French school, both the odd- and even-numbered entrechats end on two feet. The difference between the two is found in the actual execution of the beats. For an entrechat trois, French style, the dancer stands in fifth position in a demi-plié with the right foot forward. As she jumps into the air, she first beats the right foot in front (usually by crossing it over almost imperceptibly) and then proceeds to do a changement. For an entrechat quatre, she jumps into the air and crosses first to the back. In other words, for the French school, all the odd-numbered entrechats cross first to the front, while the even-numbered entrechats cross first to the back.

Grand jeté

In the entrechat quatre Russian style, the dancer starts from fifth position in demi-plié with the right foot front. As she jumps into the air, she crosses the right foot to the back and then to the front before she returns to a demi-plié in fifth position. The entrechat six is more complex because the dancer does one more crossing than in the entrechat quatre, and thus lands with the left foot front. In the entrechat huit, the dancer does an additional crossing, and finishes with the right foot front—in other words, it is a double entrechat quatre without coming down! The entrechat huit is extremely difficult, and can be done only by strong male dancers. The entrechat dix exists in theory, but is hardly ever done. It is rare for a girl to do more than an entrechat six, unless she has a partner. Then there is no limit to the number of entrechats she can perform.

The Royale is another controversial term. For the Russian school, it is a changement battu where the feet beat in front before crossing—in other words, it is the same as the entrechat trois for the French school.

The historical origin of the word "Royale" is not clear. It seems to have been invented after the entrechats trois and quatre were already in use. According to one explanation, the term Royale was born during the reign of Louis XIV. Supposedly one of the king's admirers remarked that the monarch's entrechats were more "royal" than those of his dancing partners, because he crossed his feet first to the front. With all due respect to Louis's dancing skills, nobody has solved the mystery of the Royale.

The brisé, a small, "broken" jump, is another common leap with beats. A brisé could almost be defined as a flying entrechat quatre. The dancer starts in fifth position in a demi-plié with the right foot back. As she jumps, she kicks out the right foot, performs an entrechat quatre in the air, and lands in fifth position in a demi-plié with the right foot back.

The second subdivision of leaps with beats is the batterie à choc, in which the legs hit against one another in midair. The most common jump in the category is the cabriole, or goat leap (from the Latin *capra,* "goat"). In earlier times, this term was used indiscriminately to refer to all leaps with beats. Today, however, its meaning has been restricted specifically to those leaps where the fully extended legs beat against one another in midair. The cabriole is usually performed to the front or back, and often in succession. Cabriole to the second is extremely difficult, especially if the leg is held à la hauteur. Only a few male dancers are strong enough to perform cabriole à la seconde à la hauteur.

* * *

After all these complicated exercises, the dancers are panting from strain and exhaustion. Their reserve supplies of energy are rapidly dwindling. They mop their brows, fan their flushed faces and bend over to catch their breath. Class is almost over, but not quite. The last steps do not involve great endurance and great strength, but rather test muscle control. They are a type of muscular antidote to the tremendous strain that the leaps have produced. The last exercises include battement tendu and grand battement, just to make sure that after the jumps, the dancer can still summon up the ever-important control and body placement. Finally the formal révérence, or bow to the teacher, and then the class is over.

After all that exertion, one might think that these dancers would need a week's rest to recuperate. But dancers are very resilient. In all probability, most of them will be out on stage for the evening's performance. Dancers never seem to get tired of dancing. And when they do, it is a sign that their passionate love affair with ballet has come to an end.

Chapter 7

The Double Standard

Ballet is one of the few professions in which the woman is usually the undisputed star. Though hard-core feminists may argue that the male choreographer actually exploits the ballerina by casting her in a traditional, and therefore reactionary, stereotyped role, they forget, in their anger, the position of the male dancer. Until very recently, he has been the butt of rather cruel, sexist jokes. All men dancers are sissies. What red-blooded youth would want to prance around on stage in those revealing tights? Men dancers just cannot be real men. Strange as it may seem, most people instinctively consider ballet feminine, so strongly feminine that it mysteriously "transforms" all those who join its ranks.

Male dancers have not always been considered second-class citizens. As a matter of fact, when ballet first started, only men danced. As we saw, the first professional female dancer made her debut in 1691, more than a century after ballet was officially "born." Despite the presence of women on the stage, men continued to dominate the ballet scene during the entire eighteenth century. Just think of the fame of the Vestris family; both father and son were European celebrities. In the eighteenth century, the men executed complicated jumps and leaps, while the women did lots of graceful poses and gliding terre à terre steps. The men could dance better, because they were not weighted down by the heavy costumes, towering wigs and high-heeled slippers that the female dancers wore. The customary male costume included the *tonnelet,* a type of short wired puff around the hips, which vaguely resembled the modern-day tutu.

Toward the end of the eighteenth century the pendulum began to swing in favor of the women, who had, by then, started to shed their cumbersome garb. The female dancer began to concentrate on technical virtuosity. During the Romantic period, especially the so-called golden age of ballet, the ballerina succeeded in displacing her male rival from his pedestal of stardom. Romantic ballet exalted the woman, and transformed her into a frothy, ethereal sylph who floated through the air. Ballet became stubbornly feminine, and the male dancer was often totally rejected. As a matter of fact, many of the male roles in Romantic ballets were danced by women, called *danseuses en travesti*. Thérèse Elssler gained her fame by partnering her famous sister Fanny! When the male dancer was accepted, he was relegated to a position of secondary importance, supporting the ballerina on pointe and carrying her across the stage in breathtaking lifts. Thanks to the partner, there was no longer any need for the complicated flying machines that had formerly hoisted the ballerina through the air.

Though the male dancer always commanded greater respect in Russia and Denmark, even in those countries during the nineteenth century, ballet was primarily a female and feminine art form. It was not until Michel Fokine arrived in Paris in 1909 that the pendulum began to swing back in favor of the men. Fokine encouraged his male dancers to step, as it were, out of their stereotyped cliché and to dance. Nijinsky electrified his European audiences with his multiple turns and dazzling leaps.

Ted Shawn, the father of American modern dance, played a particularly important role in stimulating a healthy new interest in dance. He encouraged the inclusion of modern dance in the physical education programs of schools and colleges. In this way he hoped to stress the similarities between dance and athletics, and thereby undermine the conventional aversion toward male dancers.

Despite these attempts, the residue of Romantic prejudice still lingers on, especially among Americans who feel an instinctive distrust of male dancers. Athletes are masculine, but male dancers have to be effeminate.

Ever since Rudolf Nureyev's defection, the male dancer is beginning to arouse new interest and enthusiasm. At times he vies with the ballerina, and threatens to usurp her traditional position of prestige. This enthusiasm, however, is generally limited to the superstars, who transcend the categories reserved for average human beings. The boy in the corps de ballet and even the

male soloist in a regional company still arouse mixed feelings. How many times have I heard people say, "Yes, yes, these ballet guys really have to work hard hauling the girls around like that. You really have to be in shape to do that work. No doubt about it! But still, I'd rather have my son become a baseball player than a ballet dancer!" It just proves that lots of things change in one hundred years, but lots of other things remain the same.

* * *

Dancers, both male and female, are classified both by rank (corps de ballet, demi-soloist, soloist, and danseur or premier danseur for the male; ballerina or prima ballerina for the female) and by type. The three broad categories of dancers are the classical, the demi-character and the character. While these three categories are now less arbitrary than formerly, they offer some indication of the requirements, physical and technical, for the various roles. The classical male would be the Prince in *Swan Lake,* the Cavalier in *The Nutcracker* or the partner in the second-movement adagio of Balanchine's *Symphony in C.* These dancers should have impeccable technique, classical line in their movement and good partnering skill, which also implies height. A tall boy is technically and aesthetically a more desirable partner.

The character dancer stands at the other end of the spectrum. He must have brilliant, often spectacular technique, a magnetic personality and good acting ability, which enables him to do humorous or comic roles. Partnering is not of primary importance. Character dancers are often of short or medium height.

The demi-character dancer borrows something from the other two types of dancers. Many of his roles demand technical virtuosity as well as elegant partnering skill. The blending of two different styles was "invented" by Jean Dauberval in his famous ballet *La Fille Mal Gardée* (1789). Here the combining of the peasant and classical elements seems to celebrate the spirit of liberty that was in the air. Before Dauberval's experiment, these two dance styles had existed only as separate, distinct entities.

Today one might be tempted to add a fourth category for ballet dancers—namely, modern ballets, which often blatantly contradict the criteria of classical ballet. Still, the conventional guidelines of the three basic categories can be applied to the modern ballets too.

* * *

Since the fundamental principles of classical ballet are the same for both sexes, most of the training is coeducational. Boys and girls study together in classes taught by men or women. Despite the outward appearance of equality, it soon becomes apparent that each sex has its particular strengths and weaknesses. Some of these differences are emphasized in class. For example, the hand position for the boys differs slightly from that for the girls. Whereas the girl usually holds her hand in a delicate, expressive position, the boy extends his fingers more uniformly, and keeps his thumb closer to the palm. When the arms are in second position, the boy keeps his palms facing the floor; the girl turns her palms forward. In an arabesque, however, the palm must be facing down for both the male and the female dancer. Details, yes, but imperfect details can detract from the finished product.

The male dancer has to concentrate on three specific areas: turns, jumps and partnering. As far as turns are concerned, he has one definite advantage over the girls. He does his turns on demi-pointe, and therefore does not have to deal with the delicate problems of balance on pointe. A good male dancer should be able to do five or six turns, and in exceptional cases even more. He is expected to perform all the varieties of pirouettes, tours piqués and tours relevés. One famous male specialty is the tour relevé in second position (sometimes called tour à l'Italienne), in which he does a series of turns with his leg in second position. These turns are often used at the end of a variation. The dancer must be very careful to keep his leg in second position, and not to "travel" all over the stage.

Men are expected to excel in the aerial turns (tours sautés). The simplest kind of jumping turn is the tour en l'air. Formerly the tour en l'air was a male prerogative, but today female dancers are expected to do one aerial turn. A male dancer does two and sometimes three. The landing from an aerial turn requires excellent muscular control, and can be done on two feet, one foot or even on the knee. The last position is obviously the most difficult, since the dancer must land gently. Sometimes, however, he loses his balance and crashes down on his knee. A painful and potentially dangerous mistake!

Lately there has been a tendency to devleop new variations on the basic steps. These innovations, especially in the area of aerial turns and beats, usually require great technical ability. They represent an attempt to destroy the cliché that male dancers are effeminate. Today the male dancer is presented as a spectacular athlete who literally defies the laws of nature.

Most of the jumps that were discussed in the preceding chapter can be performed with an added turn; thus the brisé becomes the brisé en tournant, the sissonne becomes the sissonne en tournant, the assemblé becomes the assemblé en tournant, and so forth. Sometimes these turning leaps are done on the diagonal or in a circle. The effect invariably electrifies the audience.

Brisé volé en tournant demands brilliant technique and muscular control. Here the dancer completes a turn with four brisés volés. A difficult new turning jump is the revolta, in which the dancer turns over in the air. He kicks his right foot to the fourth front as he jumps, passes his bent left leg over the right leg as he executes a half turn in the air, and then, facing backward, lands on his left leg with the right leg to the fourth back.

Men are supposed to do as many beats as they can, whenever they can. For the jumping exercises in class, the men usually leave the two groups that are formed for the off barre work, and make a third group. When their turn comes, the music is played more slowly so they can do the jumping combination with beats. Sometimes a few enthusiastic females will join the men. Valiant as their attempts may be, these eager girls do not achieve the same spectacular effect. The reason is simple: the girls' leg and back muscles are constitutionally weaker. Elevation, or the ability to jump, remains predominantly a male specialty.

In order to give the boys additional practice in jumps and turns, many schools have special men's classes. Here the dancers work on the areas that have been glossed over during the coeducational classes. They can also correct individual problems, such as sloppy turnout or poor footwork. Although the male dancer does not have to develop an arched instep for pointe work, neatly pointed toes improve his line and even his elevation for the jumps. A crooked or hooked foot is extremely unattractive on stage.

In order to correct poor footwork, some boys wear special leather toe shoes. Since it is more difficult to dance in toe shoes than in ballet slippers, they have to use extra energy to do the steps. In the long run, their instep improves, their feet get stronger and their footwork becomes neater.

Although men occasionally wear these "therapeutic" toe shoes in class, pointe work remains the ballerina's domain. Occasionally a male usurper will try his luck. For example, in Paris on February 27, 1952, Michel Renault performed the first male variation on pointe and did five consecutive pirouettes on toe—alone! Although very few ballerinas can rival his turns, his success remains an isolated case. At least thus far!

In men's class, the boys are taught how to work correctly and how to avoid straining or injuring themselves. The knees and the back are their two most vulnerable spots. The knees take a lot of strain in the preparation and landing for the complicated jumps. If the boy loses his balance or does not pull up sufficiently, the knees will suffer. Though back injuries can be caused by jumps, they are usually the result of strain during partnering. These difficulties will be discussed in the next chapter.

* * *

While the boys are jumping and turning in men's class, the girls are balancing on toe, practicing turns on pointe and working on their extension in pointe class. It takes long years of devoted work and sore feet before pointe work becomes second nature. Dancing on toe is undoubtedly the most unnatural aspect of ballet. First of all, balancing one's full weight—even if the weight is only one hundred pounds—on the ten toes contradicts all the laws of nature. The feet, especially the toes, were not created to take this kind of abuse. As a result, ballerinas suffer from all types of foot problems.

Secondly, balance on toe is a very delicate matter. Standing on five little toes gives the girl a very narrow margin for error. If she falls off pointe, she falls. Unless a girl has excellent muscle control and perfect body placement, she will never be able to perform the difficult steps on toe. She must pay particular attention to her ankles, which give her extra support. If her ankles are weak and wobbly, she will fall off pointe more easily, and possibly injure herself. This explains why the second major weak spot for girls is the ankle. It takes the brunt of support when she stands on toe, but the brunt of pain when she slips!

Arm and head movements play an important part in many of the roles the ballerina is called upon to perform. Harmonious coordination of arms and the rest of the body is often the test of a good dancer, and once again proves that dancing is far more than brilliant foot and leg work. In addition to the formal arm movements, which have no meaning in themselves but are part of the classical arm vocabulary, there is a whole series of unofficial arm movements. Some are simply movements that accompany steps but lack any special meaning. For example, with the arms en couronne in high fifth position, the hands rotate on the wrists and make tiny circles. Other arm movements have a clear meaning. For example, Odette's dramatic arm fluttering stops Prince Siegfried and his hunting companions from shooting the swans.

An especially rich category of meaningful arm movements is imitation of animal gestures. A great challenge for a girl is learning how to transform herself into a winged creature, usually a bird, often a swan. Some of the most famous ballets deal with birds: *Swan Lake, The Sleeping Beauty* (Blue Bird), *The Dying Swan, The Firebird;* other winged characters appear in *La Sylphide, Giselle* (the Wilis), *Les Sylphides, Piège de Lumière,* just to mention a few. It seems that these flying creatures correspond to man's desire for lightness and grace. Although none of Marie Taglioni's choreography has survived, we do know that she created a ballet called *Le Papillon* (The Butterfly) for Emma Livry in 1860. Taglioni, the sylph par excellence, fell under the spell of those winged creatures.

A great ballerina will actually succeed in transforming her arms into wings that bend, twist and writhe. Though the movements may appear natural, it takes long hours of practice in front of the mirror before they become second nature. Teena confesses that *The Dying Swan* is unquestionably the most difficult part she has ever learned. Not because of any technical difficulties, since the dance is really three and a half minutes of patterned bourrées. Not even because of the music, which is easy to follow, or the floor patterns of the bourrées, which are tricky but by no means impossible. But because of the arms! When Teena was learning the variation, Gabriela Darvash Taub, a Rumanian choreographer and teacher who now lives in the U.S., taught it to her in installments. "You must feel the swan's wings here [as she points to Teena's back and arms], the swan's neck here [as she runs her hand over Teena's long arched neck], but most of all, the swan's agony here [as she clasps her hands to her breast]. You cannot learn how to die in one rehearsal."

As Teena worked and practiced the variation, she complained of the terrible pains that her swan wings were causing her. "I really prefer arms to wings," she joked, "but by the time I finish learning this dance, maybe I'll look better with wings."

The Dying Swan

*   *   *

For class and rehearsal, both boys and girls wear tights. Boys usually wear a white sweat shirt and black tights, which are rolled around a belt or held up by two pieces of elastic that go over the shoulders and crisscross on the back. The boys always wear a dance belt (an elastic athletic supporter), which minimizes the risk of hernias and related ills. And on their feet they have Russian-style ballet slippers—soft kid slippers with a stiff leather sole.

The girls usually wear pink or black tights, a leotard and pointe shoes (beginning and intermediate students use the same Russian ballet slippers as the men). Most full-bosomed girls prefer a bra. A dance girdle is optional, but many girls like to have one on when working with a partner; it gives an added layer of protection from rough handling. Today dancers are more individual in their dress and often flaunt "eccentric" outfits.

There are two reasons why ballet attire is tight and scanty. First of all, it allows greater freedom of movement. Secondly, it enables the spectators to see the body. In class, the entire body must be visible so that the teacher can correct mistakes, especially in body placement. On stage, of course, costumes add the final touch to a performance.

Though the teacher should be able to see the student's body, one continual point of contention is the amount of clothing students should wear. The teacher wants only the minimum, so she can watch the student's movements. The student usually wants more layers, and energetically refuses to remove them. The girls are usually more "guilty" of wearing layers of clothes. Since the muscles have to be warmed up, it is better to cover them right from the beginning of class, especially if the studio is cold. Then the muscles have to be kept warm; if the layers are removed, the muscles will get cold and possibly cramp. And there is always the weight excuse: "I want to sweat off those extra pounds on my thighs and behind, so that's why I can't take off my three pairs of tights and leg warmers."

If the layers were limited to leg warmers, the situation might be acceptable to most teachers. But dancers tend to be excessive. It is not uncommon for them to wear two leotards, a bulky sweat shirt, one pair of heavy leg warmers over their tights and then a pair of ankle warmers. Long rubber pants is a popular outfit for the New York City Ballet. These full pants hide most of the body. In addition to being unattractive, the rubber gear causes the dancer to perspire profusely. She actually leaves pools of water wherever she stands. And perfume is not enough to counteract the olfactory "delights" of rubber pants. Dancers should be careful not to overwear these pants, because the excessive perspiring can cause dehydration.

But fashions are fickle. Maybe some new star will launch a diaphanous ballet garb that will end the feud between teacher and student.

Chapter 8

The Adagio:
Boy Meets Girl

Today the adagio is such an intrinsic part of ballet that the audience would feel cheated unless the ballerina and her partner danced together. It would be almost as absurd as a romance without kisses or a spy story without suspense. And yet the adagio is a relatively recent invention. In the early stages of ballet only men and then gradually a few women performed in group and sometimes alone. Ballet was conceived as a horizontal flow of harmonious floor patterns that delighted the eye. Horizontal is perhaps the key word, because early ballet used only terre à terre steps, adding the ballon or bouncing style a good century and a half later with Blasis. This new interest in jumping meant that ballet took on vertical dimensions. The dancer could no longer be content to glide, dart or prance across the stage. He had to be able to soar into the air and defy, as it were, the laws of gravity.

The introduction of ballon marked the beginning of ballet as we know it today. From then on, the dancer had to strive to transcend the inherent limitations of his body, to challenge the laws of nature, and to perform the unnatural.

The new emphasis on the vertical aspect of ballet was the first of many "inventions" in what we could call the second chapter in the history of ballet. Pointe work was introduced to enhance the ethereal qualities of the dreamy, Romantic ballerina. Special machines were constructed to enable the dancers to jump high into the air or to fly across the stage. Finally the machines were replaced by the male partner, who supported and lifted the ballerina in steps that would otherwise have been impossible. Thus the adagio was born.

Though the term "adagio" immediately brings to mind a beautiful love dance between the ballerina and her cavalier, this is not its only meaning. Musically, "adagio" refers to a slow tempo. "Adagio," as we have already seen, describes those slow, flowing, yet controlled exercises that test the dancer's balance, extension and coordination. The adagio can be performed at the barre or in the center of the practice studio. Nowadays it is rare to find an adagio for one dancer in a ballet, but during the nineteenth century it was quite common. One of the most famous is the graveyard adagio in the second act of *Giselle* (1841), where the peasant girl's ghost performs a hauntingly beautiful sequence that climaxes in an arabesque penchée with the hands crossed at the breast. There is an adagio for one in the Slavic theme of *Coppélia* (1870), in *La Korrigane* (1880), as well as in some new ballets—*Etudes* (1948), *Symphonie Concertante* (1947).

The adagio for two is, however, certainly more spectacular, since it enables the ballerina to perform steps that would be impossible without the support from her partner. Though the pas de deux, or the adagio for two, is today synonymous with love—and even with sensuality and sexuality in the modern ballets—it originated as a dialogue between two dancers. The first record we have of an adagio is in Charles Didelot's famous ballet, *Zéphyr et Flore*. Didelot, a pupil of the well-known Dauberval, presented this ballet in 1796 at the Royal Theater in Drury Lane. He had the English mechanics build special machines so that his dancers could fly the length and width of the stage, not just rise into the air. These lifts, though mechanical, were essential to the choreography since Didelot wanted Flore to be literally swept away by Zéphyr. It is quite probable that the ballerina stood on pointe in this ballet, but once again, with support from the flying machines.

Most important of all, however, is Didelot's introduction of the pas de deux as dialogue. Here the choreographer exploited to the maximum the difference in movements between the male and female dancers. Movement, for him, was synonymous with the dancer's natural ability to express himself. Didelot felt that the woman should embody lightness and daintiness, while the man should symbolize strength and power.

The pas de deux soon became an important part of the balletic vocabulary. During the Romantic era, when the emphasis was on the female, the male dancer was soon recognized as a superior (and certainly more economical)

A pose from Agon

substitute for the complicated flying machines. His sole function was to support, raise and balance the ballerina. Ideally he should have been invisible, but since that was not possible, he was supposed to be as inconspicuous as possible. In many ballets, as we have seen, he was often replaced by the female *danseuse en travesti,* who fulfilled his "craning" functions without defiling the femininity of ballet.

Petipa, the great French choreographer who relaunched ballet in Russia, was responsible for developing the adagio into a love duet. The lifts, or portés, became an important part of the adagio. This new, stylized love duet had to adhere to the aesthetic rules of classical ballet.

With Serge Diaghilev, the role of the male dancer in the pas de deux was expanded so that he enjoyed almost the same importance as the ballerina. Here the aesthetic harmony of the adagio depended on the complementary lines of the male and the female dancers.

Ever since the age of Petipa, the adagio has been symbolic of love. In all the great classical ballets, from *Swan Lake* to *The Sleeping Beauty,* there is inevitably a handsome prince who dotes on his beautiful princess. Love, though sometimes stylized, as in *The Nutcracker* or *Raymonda,* is the basis of the pas de deux. But it is chaste love, sometimes suffering but never sensual—though Petipa occasionally added a drop of sensuality in characters like Odile, the Black Swan. Only in more recent times has sensuality and even sexuality entered ballet. Sometimes the classically chaste pas de deux is transformed into neoclassical sensuality, as in the famous pas de deux from Balanchine's *Agon;* sometimes it becomes pure aggressive sexuality, as in Robbins's *The Cage* or in the famous seduction scene of Balanchine's *The Prodigal Son.*

Today the adagio offers one of the richest fields for balletic invention. It enables the choreographer to experiment with an entire series of new poses, new lifts, new jumps and new turns. Recently there has been an increasing tendency to stress the acrobatic elements in the adagio, even at the risk of sacrificing classical criteria. The new, often exotic poses and steps that Balanchine has used in his abstract neoclassical ballets could provide a new chapter on the expressive potential of adagio.

* * *

The two most exciting times for an aspiring ballerina are the moment she dons her first pair of shiny pink toe shoes and, later on, her first adagio class.

Pirouette with partner ending in cambré

Initially both experiences are traumatic. Her feet sting in those pink shoes, her ankles wobble as she tries to balance on both toes, her arms pump nervously in a vain attempt to improve her shaky balance. But as time goes on, she gets stronger, and she forgets that "historic" first day.

Her first adagio class is equally awkward. She falls off her pirouettes and misses her jumps. She suffers all the more because she knows what she should look like but sees in that ever-revealing mirror how she actually appears. Again she tastes the beginner's bitter dust, and either perseveres or quits. But once she is accepted in a ballet company, she can look back and laugh at those two exciting yet exasperating moments. Her awkwardness now seems quaintly amusing, because time wears the edge off all the painful experiences.

Teena laughingly recalls her first adagio class with Anatole Oboukhoff, one of the best-loved teachers at the School of American Ballet. Oboukhoff always bellowed or growled in class—actually nobody ever knew what his normal voice sounded like. Though all the students knew that his bark was worse than his bite, he still succeeded in infusing a sense of holy terror-cum-respect in his students.

The first part of Teena's adagio class went so well that she began to feel confident—almost overconfident. Oboukhoff smiled paternally at her eager attempts, and barked a few corrections at her nervous partner. Teena was not at all afraid as Oboukhoff explained how to do a shoulder lift. Here the girl was supposed to jump up as the boy lifted her to his shoulder, where she should sit regally with her arms held over her head. "Girls, jump!" shouted Oboukhoff. "Boy cannot do all work! *J-u-m-p!*" And so Teena jumped, but in her eagerness to obey Oboukhoff's orders, she jumped too high and with too much force. Her poor, inexperienced partner did not expect this extra assistance as he hoisted her up to his shoulder. The force of their combined efforts was so strong that Teena never landed on his shoulder, but started to slide down his back, behind first. As Teena cried out in fear and amazement, her terrified partner grabbed her calves to stop her from crashing to the floor. But the emergency stop so jarred Teena that her head and torso fell backward. When Oboukhoff reached them—this would-be lift happened in a matter of seconds—Teena was dangling upside down with her head bumping against her partner's buttocks. "What you do?" screamed Oboukhoff. "You no lift sack of potatoes. You lift girl!"

As soon as Teena had been rescued from her humiliating failure, she staggered away, wishing that adagio had never been invented. But Oboukhoff grabbed her arm. "Come here, miss! I show you shoulder lift." So poor Teena, flustered and flushed from her recent aerial adventure, was forced to do correct shoulder lifts under Oboukhoff's attentive eyes. "If Mr. Oboukhoff had not made me do those lifts, I would probably have been afraid to try them again. He didn't even give me time to be afraid. But that's why he was such a great teacher."

Adagio classes abound in exciting adventures. Some may be humorous, but others are dangerous. A girl who falls from a lift can really hurt herself. If a boy does not give her enough support as she comes down into a plié after a big jump, she will land too hard. The lucky dancer will feel only hot flashes of excruciating pain; an unlucky one may damage—or even snap—her Achilles tendon. If the tendon snaps, it literally curls up, just like a snapped rubber band. And a snapped Achilles tendon means no more dancing—ever. So the risks are high, and both proper training and careful supervision are imperative for those early adagio classes.

*　*　*

The key to adagio is the harmonious effect both dancers create. In other words, how the boy partners the girl is just as important as what she does. A

Développé with partner

partner who drags or pushes the girl inevitably destroys the magical effect of her movements. The desired harmonious impression is produced not only by smooth, seemingly effortless coordination between the two dancers, but also by the lines created by their joint movements. This means that there must be a certain balance between what they both do. This visual harmony can be achieved in three ways. They can do the same movement—but this immediately eliminates all the steps in which the male supports or lifts the female. They can perform symmetrical movements—but here again, the aerial dimension of the adagio is excluded. Finally, they can execute steps in which their combined movements create a harmonious whole. This, of course, is the most frequent solution, since it enables the choreographer to exploit the wealth of possibilities in the adagio.

The vocabulary of the adagio is extensive, because it includes all the steps the dancer can perform alone, those very same steps performed with support from the partner, as well as a series of new steps that can be performed only with the help of the partner. To give one example, the poses are the same whether the dancer performs them in an adagio or in a solo. The steps are also the same, and may be performed with the leg tendu or plié, with the foot à plat, sur la demi-pointe or sur la pointe, with the arms in one of the five classical positions, etc. But in the adagio there are two additional possibilities which can be done only with support. A pose may be pushed (poussé) or drawn out (étiré). For an arabesque poussée, the partner pushes the axis of the girl's body forward, so that the distance between the supporting and the extended leg is reduced. In an arabesque étirée, the movement is reversed. The axis of the body is shifted backward, and therefore the back leg is extended high, almost in a split. Unlike the arabesque poussée, which is a rather intimate pose, this position is spectacular. Both the pushed and the drawn-out poses can be done only if a partner supports the girl.

The supporting positions in the adagio are varied, but there are two basic divisions. The girl may use the boy for support, holding on to one or both of his hands, or leaning on his arm, shoulder, waist, leg or neck for additional support. This type of support can be used for extension, balance, turns and occasionally jumps, but not lifts (except in a few special cases).

The second—and more versatile—method is for the boy to hold on to the girl. Usually he holds her by one or two hands in any of the classical positions (and for the modern ballets, in practically any position) or by the waist. For the lifts, he can hold on to practically any part of her anatomy to achieve the desired effect. For example, he may hold one hand under her waist and the other under her leg in arabesque and raise her into the air. Or she may be literally balanced on his hands, which support her pelvis as she "lies" on her stomach in the air with her feet extended. In many of these spectacular new semi-acrobatic poses, the girl is literally at her partner's mercy. Once she has taken her pose, he raises her high into the air. She can only hold her pose, and hope all goes well. If the boy makes a mistake, weakens or miscalculates, she falls. It takes a lot of courage and a strong dose of trust in one's partner.

Sometimes these spectacular lifts are combined with jumps or throws. The girl will be raised into a pose, thrown into the air and caught again in the same or a different pose. Or she will run at her partner from a distance and jump into his arms, usually in a spectacular pose. I secretly rejoiced when Teena admitted that it took her a long while to gain enough courage to do a fish (poisson). For this step and its infinite variations, the partner holds one

Arabesque étirée

hand on the girl's waist and the other under her thigh, and drops her forward as she arches her back. The starting position for a fish may be a stationary pose or a jump. Being overly cautious by nature, I had never dared to jump and end in a fish. I preferred to accept, as graciously as I could, my "fraidy-cat" status rather than risk a broken nose or worse. But I envied Teena's pluck as she whipped through those hair-raising lifts. One day, however, she confessed to me that the fish had really put her courage to the test. "I just couldn't jump into a dive and trust that boy. As I looked at him from across the room, I wondered if he'd really be able to do it. After all, he was still learning and I didn't want him to experiment on my body. I don't have any spare parts." After Teena finally overcame this psychological barrier and did her fish, she felt relieved, "because I had finally done it, but above all because I had lived through it."

Ballet, or maybe dance in general, is a strange mixture of body, mind and spirit, but nobody knows how much of each you need to be a good dancer—

probably because the correct dosage varies from person to person and from step to step. What is sure, however, is that a dancer can never be ruled by his mind alone. The mind must work, but never control the situation. If it did, the mind might even order the body to stop all those unnatural, painful and even dangerous movements. This hesitation would be fatal, since it overlooks the basic premise of dance—namely, that the beauty in dance consists precisely in transcending the human limitations of the body. As Mr. Balanchine likes to repeat to his dancers: "Don't think, just do!"

*　　*　　*

In the adagio there are three basic types of movements: the pas à terre, or the steps done on the ground, such as extension, pirouettes, relevés, etc.; the sauts, or jumps; the portés, or lifts. Naturally, these three movements are combined into a variety of patterns, and are thus interdependent. The jumps, in particular, serve as preparation for the lifts.

As we have already seen, these movements belong to two general categories —those that the ballerina can perform either by herself or with support from her partner, and those that can be done only with the partner. The pas à terre and the sauts belong to the first category. Alone the ballerina can perform a grand rond de jambe to an arabesque penchée or pirouettes en dehors, but with a partner's support she can make these movements more spectacular. For example, she can do the grand rond de jambe on pointe rather than à plat and end in a perfect arabesque penchée. Or she can do an infinite number of pirouettes on pointe as long as her partner turns her and makes sure she does not fall off toe. She can also end the pirouettes in an arabesque on pointe rather than in the usual plié. In other words, partnering adds a dramatic element to ballet, and arouses the audience's enthusiasm.

The portés clearly belong to the second category. They constitute the distinctive element of the adagio. In the portés the ballerina no longer belongs to the world of normal human beings. She is a free spirit who floats and flies through the air. She is not weighted down by the laws of gravity. She makes the unnatural seem beautiful, effortless and almost natural.

Though the ballerina may appear weightless and the partner may show no apparent strain, the visual effect is an illusion. No matter how thin the girl is, she weighs more than ninety pounds. No matter how strong the boy is, he has

The fish

to build up strength and endurance for the adagio. Partnering is hard work, which requires complementary coordination and muscle control from both dancers. The boy has to be strong enough to be able to lift and hold the girl in all the portés. He must also be sensitive to her equilibrium so that he can gently, almost imperceptibly, get her back on balance. For example, during multiple pirouettes, he not only turns her by the waist, but also moves her back if she begins to veer to one side. In other words, a good partner can "save the show," and make the ballerina do wonders, while a poor partner can make even the greatest star look like a novice.

Though the boy's strength and sensitivity to the girl's balance are fundamental to the adagio, they are not enough to transform a weak, sloppy dancer into a *prima ballerina assoluta*. The girl must be strong and must help her partner. She cannot expect him to lift her dead weight. For example, she should do a plié and jump exactly when he starts to lift her. In this way, the force of her preparation will "propel" the lift, and make it look smooth and effortless. Unless the two movements coincide, the lift—if it succeeds—will be jerky, low and sloppy.

Theoretically a small, thin girl should be the easiest to partner. First of all, there is less of her to move, and secondly, her equilibrium is less delicate. As all children know, it is easier to balance a small top than a large one. There are, however, exceptions to every rule. Sometimes a dancer is hard to work with because she "fights" her partner, instinctively tightening up, and thus becoming heavier and more difficult to move. Contradictory as it may seem, "heaviness" rarely has to do with weight, because ballerinas have to be thin. It usually results from the inability to relax and follow the boy. An everyday analogy can be found in dancing—the "romantic" dances where the boy holds his girl close, not those frantic, kinky do-your-own-thing affairs. Some girls simply do not want to follow their partner, and try instead to lead him. And as a result, some of the romance is lost, because neither wants to follow the leader.

Partnering is not only difficult but also painful. The boy feels considerable muscle strain, especially in his back. Excessive strain can sometimes produce hernias. The girl also feels physical pain in the adagio, since she is literally handled, thrown and caught by the boy. While a good partner tries not to maul the girl, he has to hold on to her securely during a lift, or catch her firmly after a throw. After all, he does not want her to fall.

A boy may be rough for a variety of reasons. If his hands are sweaty, the girl may slip, and as a consequence he may have to grab her roughly to stop her from falling. In order to minimize these risks, he will often rub rosin into the palms of his hands. He may not be conscious of his strength. Or he may become nervous, and react by grabbing the girl and holding on to her, possibly a bit too tightly for her comfort.

During rehearsal, the girl can cry out in pain and even curse her partner, but during performance she should not let the audience know that her partner twisted her arm or dug his fingers into her waist. Sometimes it is impossible to hide the mistake. If a boy catches a girl on the rib cage and not on the waist, her involuntary gasp will cause the audience to gasp too, thereby breaking the spell of the adagio.

Although Teena wears a variety of leotards, leg warmers, ankle warmers, tights and sweat shirts during class, she peels off many layers, especially the sweat shirts, for adagio rehearsal. "It's too dangerous," she points out, "be-

Cambré with shift of body axis.

cause the boy cannot feel where you are under all those layers of clothing. And if he grabs your sweat shirt instead of your waist when you begin to lose balance, you'll probably fall."

Since harmonious coordination is the key to good partner work, the boy and girl should practice under conditions that simulate performance. On stage a girl usually wears a costume—a tutu or long skirt—though sometimes a simple leotard is worn for the modern ballets. Most of the movements "feel" different in a costume. When the girl wears a tutu, the boy has to stand farther away from her because of the added width of the skirt. If they do a shoulder lift, he has to expect the skirt to be crushed against his face. For the difficult adagios, many ballerinas like to wear a practice tutu—just the ruffled skirt which has been detached from the satin bodice—during rehearsal in order to avoid unpleasant surprises in performance.

Although a leotard on stage is the least complicated costume, it involves certain aesthetic risks, which are greatly increased during adagio work. The legs of the leotard tend to ride up, especially when a boy throws and catches the girl. Nothing is more unattractive than a ballerina with her derrière hanging out of the leotard. "And worst of all," asserts Teena, "it makes your behind look big and fat"—anathema for every dancer! Therefore, most girls tack the legs of the leotard to their tights, as well as pin their bra straps to the shoulders of the leotard. Personal appearance is very important on stage.

Bruising, though unavoidable, is perhaps the least serious of the professional hazards of partnering. Practicing a difficult lift over and over produces bruises. When Teena does an adagio with lifts in arabesque, her under-thighs bear the prints of her partner's fingers. Strains, pulls, sprains are almost a normal part of the dancer's life. Broken ribs are relatively common, and can cause serious rifts between the ballerina and her partner. While the boy is usually at fault, sometimes his only alternative to catching the ballerina too roughly is dropping her. But the reference to the alternative sounds like a paltry excuse when the ballerina faces several weeks of forced inactivity. Unfortunately there have been cases of serious, even irreparable, injuries during adagio work—broken bones, snapped Achilles tendons, back problems.

Many friends ask Teena if she is afraid of the adagio work. "Well, sometimes," she sighs, "but life is really one big risk. You don't have to be doing the *Corsaire* adagio to get hurt. It's been statistically proven that most accidents occur at home." There may even be a kernel of truth in Teena's quasi-philosophical justification. I do not know of any statistical analysis of the injury rate among dancers, but I do know—and popular hearsay would support me—that most dancers live to a ripe old age.[1] Whether or not the two things are related is perhaps a question of personal interpretation.

Chapter 9

Preparing for the Performance

The year that Teena was asked to join the New York City Ballet company, I was studying at the University of Rome. I can still remember all the details of that exciting day. I went to my morning classes at the university, just like any other ordinary Tuesday. I fought the midday rush hour traffic on my way back to the house where I was living with a tiny wisp of an eighty-two-year-old *signora*. I had no sooner opened the door than the maid, Vera, came rushing up to me. "Thank goodness, you've finally arrived, *signorina!*" she gasped in a flutter of excitement. "Your mother is calling again at two-fifteen. She said it was *very* important." It was quite obvious to me, even in my anticipation of speaking with my parents, that a phone call from the United States was a major event in Vera's monotonous life.

The old *signora* and I only picked at the tasty lunch that Vera had prepared. We were waiting for that magic ring. When the call finally came through, over an hour late, both the *signora* and Vera were taking their usual afternoon siesta. My mother told me the good news, and I screamed with joy, rudely rousing the two sleeping ladies from their afternoon dreams. Though the *signora* usually demanded complete silence from three to five—no typing, no radio, no loud talking on the phone—she overlooked my thoughtless behavior because of this special phone call from *la mia Mamma*. In Italy, as everyone knows, motherhood is a sacred institution that commands respect, even in international relations.

*   *   *

When I returned to the United States for my senior year at Sarah Lawrence College, Teena was no longer a starry-eyed novice in the company. She had acquired an aura of professionalism that made me feel young and childish. I was embarrassed, sometimes even ashamed, that I was only a college student with no precise plans for my future, while my kid sister was an exotic artist with a job and a real salary. I found myself in the ironic position of being the big sister suffering from a little sister's inferiority complex, and tried to bury my feelings of guilt in Dante's *Inferno*.

Indeed, Teena was very professional after nine months in the company, but I overlooked the fact that her new self-confidence had not come naturally. Experience had taught her a lot. In the ballet world, you just do not survive unless you learn quickly. Like all forms of show business, ballet means lots of hard work in a ruthlessly competitive world that gives no quarter to the weak. You either make it, or you don't. "Almost" is a word that does not exist in ballet lingo.

*   *   *

The preparations for a performance are a lot more complex than most people imagine. Leaving aside all the technical details of scenery, lighting, props and special effects, which are the responsibility of the stage manager and his specialized crew, the finished performance involves hours of rehearsals. It is virtually impossible to teach a new ballet to all the dancers at once. The usual procedure is to teach small workable segments of the ballet, first to the corps and then to the principals. They will rehearse together only when every dancer knows his or her part. Then the choreographer can correct important details like spacing, correct lines and symmetrical movements during the full company rehearsal. These rehearsals are particularly important in ballets where the corps performs lots of weaving patterns around the ballerina and her partner. Sometimes a girl accidentally bumps into the ballerina and causes her to lose her balance. Depending on the temperament of the ballerina, the reaction will run from a sharp "Watch out next time, will you!" to a

Resting a moment before performance

loud string of four-letter invective that makes a new member cringe with fear and an old pro snort with rage.

During the rehearsals, two or three dancers (the number depends on the size of the ballet) are cast as understudies, who can step in at the last moment in cases of illness or injury. Since it would be far too complicated and costly to have a substitute for every corps role, the understudies are supposed to learn various places. For example, one understudy may be expected to learn the parts of all the girls on the right, while the second covers the girls on the left. Most dancers find it relatively easy to do another position in the corps as long as the steps are performed to the same side. When a dancer has to switch sides and work to the left instead of the right, the chances of her making a mistake greatly increase.

Despite the ballet mistress's efforts to have sufficient understudies, there are unavoidable emergencies. The "accident rate" tends to increase on tour or at the end of a hard season, and a girl may be "thrown into a part" at the last minute. Sometimes she may not even have a full rehearsal with the other dancers. Once Teena had to learn *Allegro Brillante* in an hour, because one of the girls had twisted her ankle. While dancers are expected to learn quickly, it is almost impossible to learn a twenty-minute ballet in such a short time. Since Teena was not the first girl, she could watch the dancer in front of her, and listen to the cues that the others called out to her. Unknown to the audience, dancers can and do talk on stage, especially in emergency situations. While Teena's fill-in performance may not have been technically perfect, the show went on. And that is what really matters. Most of the audience probably did not notice the skinny, dark-haired girl whose eyes were glued on the other dancers.

Although rehearsals are essential for the success of a ballet, they exhaust the dancers. Repeating a difficult sequence over and over until the ballet mistress is satisfied with the spacing, timing and phrasing of the movements is physically and psychologically depleting. In order to assure the dancers a minimum of protection against overwork, there are rather strict union rules for rehearsing. If there is no performance, a dancer may be scheduled for as many as eight hours of rehearsal, but no more than three consecutive hours without at least a one-hour break. Five hours of rehearsal time is considered a "normal" schedule. For the extra three hours, which a dancer is legally bound to attend, she receives overtime pay. During the season, the legal number of rehearsal hours is reduced to five—two of which are considered "normal," while the other three constitute overtime. Once again, a dancer may legally refuse to do more than three consecutive hours of rehearsal. Since rehearsing is a costly affair, most companies try to keep rehearsal time within the maximum number of legal hours. It usually happens that the choreographer's new or favorite ballets take up most of the rehearsal time, while the old standards get a cursory run-through.

* * *

The behind-the-scenes preparations for a performance involve much more than rehearsals. Most ballets, except the very modern ones, use costumes. The dancers are sent for special fittings because the costumes are custom made. These fittings are important for two reasons. First of all, the choreographer must be satisfied with the finished effect. Secondly, the dancers must be able to move and bend with a minimum of discomfort—although there are many disagreements between the costume designer and the dancers about where comfort ends and discomfort begins. Sometimes both the designer and the choreographer overlook important details. When Teena went down to Madame Karinska's to be fitted for her "Diamonds" costume ("Diamonds" is the third ballet in Balanchine's trilogy, *Jewels*), Mr. B. happened to be there. He inspected her glittering white costume, which was literally encrusted with rhinestones. The satin bodice stopped under the bosom, which was scantily draped with a thin veil of flesh-colored tulle and an occasional "diamond." The total effect was dazzling, and Mr. B. seemed pleased.

A few days later, Teena was called down to Madame Karinska's for another "Diamonds" fitting. She was a trifle perplexed, because Mr. B. had so enthusiastically praised Karinska's lavish creation. As soon as Teena tried on her costume, however, the mystery was solved. The plunging, Cretan-inspired neckline had been ideal for flat-chested girls like Teena, but unfortunately vulgar for anyone with a full bosom. The all-to-revealing neckline was raised, so that the dancing Diamonds would not tempt the audience with their natural jewels.

It takes a while to get used to dancing in a costume. At first the dancer may feel restricted by the tight bodice, the elastic straps that pull on her shoulders, or the puffy, wired skirt of the tutu. As we saw, adagio work becomes more difficult with a costume. When the girl wears a tutu, the boy has to stand farther away; when she wears a long chiffon skirt, he has to be careful not to get tangled in the yards of material or to step on it.

After several months, both the tutu—either the traditionally classical model or the longer version—and the long skirt become second nature to the ballerina. But there are other costumes which the dancers never learn to like. For example, the Spanish dress in the "Hot Chocolate" variation of Balanchine's *The Nutcracker* weighs approximately ten pounds. Its weight tires the girl's back, and lifts, turns and jumps require extra effort. But most important of all, the girl must remember that the heavy skirt moves after her, not with her. This added momentum makes it extremely difficult to change directions, because she has to summon up double energy to move both her body and her skirt.

Probably the most difficult costume in Teena's career was the long black-and-gold dress for the court sequence in Balanchine's version of *Don Quixote*. The costume was historically authentic, with its long velvet hoop skirt, high ruffled neckpiece and imposing hat. The stately court dance had seemed like child's play until the full dress rehearsal. "We couldn't breathe in those costumes, let alone move!" recalls Teena. The regal effect of the stylized movements was spoiled as one of the black-clad ladies slowly fell backward. In the midst of all that gold and velvet, the audience—the Friends of the Ballet, who are privileged to attend one dress rehearsal—saw a pair of thin pink legs thrashing wildly in the air. The dancers on stage heard a muffled "Help, help! Get me out of here!" Mr. B. immediately stopped the rehearsal to rescue the dancer in distress.

Teena had fallen because she was unaccustomed to moving in her new costume. When she had stepped backward, she miscalculated, forgetting that the heavy skirt would move after her. As a result, she stepped on the skirt and lost her balance. The forward momentum of the skirt actually pulled her over backward. As poor Teena fell slowly and painlessly to the floor, the large hoop skirt settled down over her upper body like a giant parachute. It took two strong boys to get her back on her feet.

The costumes for a ballet are very expensive since they are handmade. A plain, classical tutu costs about four hundred dollars. If this figure seems excessive, just take into consideration the satin bodice, which fits like a corset, and the skirt, which consists of twelve layers of graduated, scalloped net, sometimes held up by a wire hoop. The bodice is specially attached to the net skirt, so that there is enough "give" for the dancer to bend and stretch without ripping the costume. The shoulder straps are made of soft, flesh-colored elastic, which allow the ballerina to move without fear of losing her costume. Since the corps de ballet often alternates parts in the various ballets, the costumes are used by more than one dancer. Each costume has three rows of hooks. Sometimes the body variations among the dancers are such that the wardrobe mistress has to make minor alterations—a strip of satin sewn along the rows of hooks to add an extra inch to the bodice, a strip of net in the panties to lengthen the crotch, bust pads to fill out the bosom, darts or seams to reduce the circumference of the bodice.

A professional dancer soon learns that she must take good care of the costumes. There is a whole series of unofficial rules that the newcomer quickly discovers. First of all, a dancer puts on her costume just a few minutes before going on stage. The wardrobe mistress and her assistants watch carefully over their costumes as if they were small, helpless children. A dancer should not sit down or lean against the scenery for fear of tearing or soiling her costume. Since it is the wardrobe mistress's responsibility to keep the costumes in good shape, she naturally wants to reduce extra work. As it is, she has to spot-clean the costumes after each performance, and clean them thoroughly (this means detaching the skirt from the bodice, washing the net skirt, cleaning the bodice with cleaning fluid and reassembling the entire costume) before they get too dirty. The costumes become soiled from perspiration and from both the girl's and boy's make-up. In general, the boys wear a dark base, which leaves brown smudges on the light, frothy tutus. Besides which, they often rub rosin on their hands to minimize the risks of "sweaty" hands in adagio work. The rosin, of course, soils the ballerina's costume.

If the costumes are not spot-cleaned regularly, they become too dirty to be used on stage, and have to be replaced. Dancers who are careless or sloppy with their costumes may be fined; usually they are warned beforehand. When a costume is damaged or badly soiled during performance, the wardrobe mistress repairs or cleans it immediately. If a dancer is doing a guest performance with another company, she is personally responsible for the costume, unless, of course, it belongs to her. Once Teena had to pay a twenty-five-dollar cleaning bill because the costume she had borrowed from the New York City Ballet was so badly stained from her partner's dark make-up and dirty hands.

An ironic reversal of convention, whereby the male is customarily responsible for all money transactions.

When the company goes on tour, the dancers do not have to worry about carrying their own costumes. Each dancer is even given a theater case, which she fills with her backstage essentials such as tights, leotards, make-up, a sewing kit, extra ribbons and elastics, a wrap for the theater, and the like. The company sends each dancer's theater case along with the costumes and scenery, and delivers it to the dressing rooms in the various theaters.

For guest performances, however, the star has to bring her own costume, shoes, make-up and other accessories. A tutu is difficult to transport because of its bulk—certainly not its weight. It cannot be packed into a suitcase, or squashed under the airplane seat. It must be carried by hand, and hung in such a way that the skirt is not crushed. On a plane, a tutu can send the stewardesses into a tizzy. Last Christmas, when Teena was going to Dallas for a guest performance of *The Nutcracker,* she had some difficulty because of her tutus. Actually, she had taken along two, just in case something happened. "Better be on the safe side," Teena explains, "because you cannot run down to the nearest Woolworth's and buy another tutu."

The economy section of the plane was jammed with people going back to see their families for the holidays. There was not one extra seat, and of course, no place for the tutus: under the seat was out of the question, the overhead compartments were too small, the two closets were stuffed. Teena could not even hold the tutus in her lap, because aside from the discomfort it would have caused her seat partners, it was against airline safety regulations. Fortunately one helpful stewardess whisked the tutus into the first-class compartment, where there happened to be two free seats. She fastened the seat belts around each of them, so they would not be in danger of flying out of the seats. The problem tutus actually received better treatment than their owner!

Though tutus are bulky to carry, they do, upon occasion, create humorous situations. Because of her numerous trips abroad for dancing engagements, Teena is now a familiar figure to some U.S. customs officers. The first time she carried her costume back, the officer insisted on opening the suspicious-looking garment bag containing her tutu. He blinked in amazement as she carefully extracted a beautiful "diamond"-encrusted costume, which looked strangely out of place in that stark, neon-lit room. Teena explained that she had been dancing in Europe, and had to bring her own costume. And now every time Teena comes back to the U.S., she seems to meet her friend, who is always anxious to inspect—curiosity only—her latest costume. The officer has even nicknamed her "Tutu Teena"!

*   *   *

While most companies give their dancers a fixed number of free toe shoes, it is each dancer's responsibility to prepare the shoes for the performance. Preparing shoes means more than sewing on the ribbons and elastics; it means more than breaking in the shoes, just to the right point, for each ballet. Preparing the shoes sometimes means dyeing them to match the yellow tights or emerald green skirt. While pink is the most common color, the dancers usually request a few pairs in white and black. White shoes are a must for the so-called white ballets like *Swan Lake* or the "Diamonds" section in *Jewels*. White shoes are also easier to dye than pink ones. Black shoes, on the other hand, are required for certain roles—Balanchine's *Western Symphony* or Taras's *Ebony Concerto*. Although it is possible to dye pink or white shoes black, the dye from the shoes and ribbons stains the dancer's feet. It is hardly attractive to have black feet and black ribbon marks on the ankles.

The ballet company has a special dye box, where the dancer can mix the required color and then dye her shoes and ribbons. The dyeing process should be done well before performance, so that the shoes can dry thoroughly. In order to speed up the process, the shoes are sometimes placed in the "hot box," a kind of small electric oven. The dye, however, makes the shoes shrink and the ribbons become stiff. As a result, most girls hate dancing with dyed shoes. "And in addition to the discomfort of shrinkage," complains Teena, "it takes days to get that terrible dye off your feet and ankles, because the skin literally drinks up the color!"

Since the number of free shoes a dancer receives is not unlimited, she has to be economical with them. Generally she will save the "good" new shoes for a particularly important or difficult performance. Although each girl has her shoes made according to precise specifications, there are inevitable differences among the pairs because they are made by hand, by different artisans. When

Teena gets a new shipment of shoes, she always tries on every pair to sort out the "good" ones from the "bad" ones. She makes cryptic marks on the soles to remind herself when to wear what pair.

But preparing shoes for a performance does not mean only preparing the "good" new pairs. It means alternating the "good" ones and then letting them dry out. A shoe becomes soft from use—and abuse—but also from the heat of the feet. If dried out, the shoe will "harden up," not to its original stiffness, but enough to be used for a less demanding ballet. Some girls even put soft, "sweaty" shoes in the hot box to harden them up.

In addition to drying out the older shoes—they are usually hung around the light bulbs that circle the dancer's make-up mirror—the dancer must also clean them. Loose ribbon ends and dirty toe shoes are the true signs of a nonprofessional. The toe shoes may be brushed to remove superficial dust and rosin, and then dabbed with cleaning fluid to remove the stubborn spots.

Probably the most important preparatory aspect of the toe shoe routine is the almost unconscious ribbon and elastic check. A detached ribbon can really compromise a dancer's performance, or even cause her to trip. And the few moments on stage are too precious to be wasted.

*   *   *

Everybody knows that a dancer has to put on make-up for a performance. Without make-up, the audience would not be able to see the dancer's facial expressions, which constitute an important part of her dancing. Make-up is supposed to accent the key spots in the face—especially the eyes and the mouth—but it can also correct facial flaws. For example, a girl with a round, puffy face often puts brown shading under her cheekbones for a leaner look. Another dancer may use a thin strip of white shading down the middle of her nose and then add a line of brown on either side. This striped effect will "slenderize" a wide, fat nose. The basic principle is to use dark shading on areas that you want to reduce or shorten, and white shading on areas you want to emphasize.

Today's stage make-up is not as heavy as it used to be. The desired effect on stage is natural, except, of course, in special character roles. While most girls prefer false eyelashes to thick mascara or wax beading, they avoid the bright blue eye shadow and rigidly drawn eyebrows that characterized the ballerinas of fifteen years ago. The shades of lipstick vary, but traffic-light red has generally lost its appeal. Girls with large, strong mouths prefer the earthy shades, which minimize the size of their mouths.

Most girls avoid wearing body make-up unless they are doing very special, classical roles. Body make-up is difficult to apply, but even worse to remove. Nothing is more tedious than creaming off body make-up after a tiring performance. And yet it has to be removed, or else it will soil the girl's street clothes, and eventually ruin her skin. A little trick that Teena uses when she wants to avoid using body make-up is sprinkling herself with talcum powder. The powder does not harm the skin and actually absorbs some of the perspiration. Furthermore, under the spotlights it gives the body a soft, smooth look. Best of all, it washes off with soap and water.

The boys have to put on make-up, but theirs is less complicated than the girls'. They usually apply a dark base, which gives them a masculine look. They darken their eyebrows and outline their eyes. Lipstick, false eyelashes and rouge are out of the question.

The dancers in the New York City Ballet all do their own make-up. Recently the company has engaged a make-up consultant who gives advice to the new dancers and does some special character make-up. The basic stage make-up can be used for all roles except the character ones. Generally the dancer touches up her face during intermission, and then is ready for the next ballet. Changing make-up from one ballet to the next is always an unpleasant process because the time is usually limited and the dancer is overheated. It is very difficult to apply make-up to a perspiring face.

* * *

Most dancers have long hair because it is easier to tie back. Once upon a time, the only hair style allowed was the so-called ballerina look—hair severely parted down the center and tied into a low bun on the nape of the neck. Today this look is definitely "out," unless the ballet happens to be a Romantic revival. The most common hair style is the high bun or the French twist. Mr. Balanchine detests buns—the low "ballerina" ones along with the high ones—because they make the head look big and lumpy. He tells all his

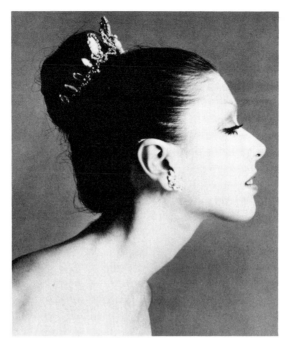

Ballerina with crown

girls to pin their hair into a French twist, which, he maintains, elongates the neck and maintains the curved shape of the head. The hair should always be pulled back tautly and rolled neatly into the twist, with no loose, flying ends. If a girl has bangs (hardly advisable!) or soft short ends, she must plaster them down with hair spray or water.

Not all ballets require the hair to be pinned back. In some modern ballets, the dancer wears a ponytail or even lets her hair hang loose. Once again, long hair is not only more practical but also more spectacular.

Very often the dancer wears a headpiece. For the Romantic ballets, it is a wreath; for the pure classical or neoclassical ones, a crown or a tiara. Other ballets may have fanciful headpieces. The first rule for headpieces is pinning them on securely. They should not flop on one's head, or come loose and fall on stage. A dancer uses lots of hairpins and bobby pins to hold the headpiece securely in place. Very often these ornaments are quite heavy. The combined weight of the headpiece and the pins frequently causes headaches and sore scalps.

The final professional touch consists of adding a bit of glitter. Huge, faceted rhinestone earrings are the answer. The sparkle of these garish ornaments is

Ballerina with tiara

picked up by the strong spotlights, and adds warmth to the dancer's face. Most dancers have a drawer full of earrings with rhinestones of varying sizes, rhinestone broaches to pin on the bodice of their costumes, rhinestone bobby pins. These gems are worn only in the hair, on the ears or on the costume; never on the neck or arms, where the glitter would be distracting.

*   *   *

Many of the practical preparations take place in the dressing room, where each girl has her own make-up place and mirror studded with light bulbs. In the corps de ballet dressing rooms, there are anywhere from eight to twenty-six girls, who chatter excitedly about the latest ballet gossip as they get ready for performance. The tone is often catty and cruel. Invariably there are the newsmongers, who relate the rich tidbits of gossip with almost sensual gusto. "So-and-so was a real disgrace in *Raymonda*. She couldn't jump, and she fell off all her pirouettes. I wonder *how* she got that part!" Jealousies and rivalries build up, and many girls fall victim to this insidious chitchat. Even today, Teena remembers the best single piece of advice she ever received. Felia

Doubrovska, one of the most elegant teachers at the School of American Ballet, told Teena never, but *never,* to listen to the dressing room gossip. "It will ruin you and your dancing," Doubrovska said, sighing. "Things haven't changed since my day."

The principals and soloists are spared the excesses of gossip and noise in their private or semiprivate rooms. Teena confesses that one of the nicest fringe benefits of becoming a soloist was the quiet dressing room where "you can get yourself psyched up for a difficult role, or just relax during intermission."

All the dressing rooms have loudspeakers, so the dancers can hear the stage calls or the music. They soon become accustomed to listening for important cues: half-hour call, when dancers must be in the theater or risk a fine for tardiness; curtain calls, intermission, five minutes (before curtain), and important announcements, which contribute to the smooth coordination of the show.

*   *   *

All the practical preparations, while long and time-consuming, would serve little purpose if the dancer did not prepare her muscles for the performance. In other words, she must do another barre before going on stage. Not as long or as strenuous a barre as the one in the morning class, but one that warms up her muscles without tiring them. The muscles must be in perfect shape for the challenge on stage.

Just how long do all these preparations, practical and muscular, really take? While the time varies from dancer to dancer, and depends greatly on the role she has to perform, a safe average would be two hours. This means that the dancer arrives at the theater around six o'clock for an eight o'clock show. Thus, for approximately fifteen minutes of actual dancing, she spends two hours getting ready. I used to think that my own ratio of three hours of "at home" preparation for one hour of classroom teaching was high, until I started figuring out the comparable ratio for the ballerina. Hers is about eight to one! But these moments of glitter on stage more than make up for the preparatory drudgery. "There's nothing like being out there on that big stage," explains Teena with a look of longing in her deep blue eyes. "It makes you forget all those hours of work and sacrifice. You have to experience it before you can really understand what I mean."

A pre-performance run-through

Chapter 10

The Performance

A few years ago I was head over heels in love with a dashing young Italian whom I had met in Florence. The mutual fascination was strong enough to make him come to New York to see, as he so carefully stated, whether the American Joanie was really any different from the Giovanna he had known in Florence. Since I wanted him to become acquainted with my world, I took him to Rutgers University, where I was teaching, to parties with my friends, to my secret haunts and favorite restaurants and, of course, to the ballet. As it was December, the only ballet we could see was *The Nutcracker,* but Christmas in New York is probably best summed up by this traditional ballet.

We sat in the orchestra, and were enchanted by the fairy-tale ballet. We laughed as the children romped during the party, sighed as the lovely Snowflakes whirled through the crystal forest, applauded as the Candy Canes leaped across the stage, hummed as the gracious pink and lilac Flowers waltzed to their familiar strains, and held our breath as the handsome Cavalier partnered the luscious Sugar Plum Fairy in a spectacular adagio. Both of us were a bit sad when the curtain dropped and broke the magic spell. Our two-hour trip to the land of sweets and delights had ended.

A few nights later, Teena told us that she had received permission for us to watch *The Nutcracker* from the wings. I knew that this would be a special experience for my Florentine, because he would be able to see the other side of ballet, the side that the audience out front never even imagines. We took our places in the first wing—the best place for watching backstage, since you can see the dancers from the front or, at worst, from the side, but rarely from the back. Viewed from this new angle, the first act did not seem radically different. Naturally, we lost the total effect of the choreographic patterns, but we enjoyed the small details that the audience could not notice. For example, we could hear the dancers occasionally chiding the children when they became unruly or nervous. There was considerable talking among the dancers during the party scene. We even heard a few bored comments, like "Only twenty-five more *Nutcracker*s to go" or "This ballet really makes me forget the joys of Christmas."

The real shock, however, came during the second act, which is pure dancing. Because of my ballet training, I knew what to expect, but my friend did not. He stared wide-eyed as the dancers strained to make their movements achieve that effortless quality. They were all perspiring profusely, panting from the long, winding sequences they had to perform and flushed from the exertion. He gasped involuntarily as one male dancer raced into the first wing and collapsed on the floor to catch his breath. He gazed in concern as he saw how the veins under the dancers' arms or in their necks swelled with the strain. During the entire second act, his body was tense and rigid as if he were trying to dance along with the performers. He did not relax until the end of the show, when the audience's resounding applause repaid the dancers for their beautiful performance.

After the show he asked me a deceptively simple question. "We've seen the same ballet twice," he said, "but in my opinion, they were really two different ballets. Which *Nutcracker* was the real one?" And his point was very well taken, because in ballet, as in all theater, for that matter, there exists a dichotomy between reality and illusion. The simplest answer to his question was, of course, that the real ballet was the one the audience saw from the front, but this answer automatically implied that the one he had seen from the wings was an illusion. That was certainly not the case, since there is nothing more "real" than the physical strain of ballet. So I amended my original answer. The audience was sheltered from the unromantic reality of ballet, because they saw the dancers from a distance and from only one perspective. But I was not satisfied with this second answer. It was tantamount to admitting that what the audience saw was indeed an illusion.

Maybe the only answer to his question is that ballet, like life, is a strange mixture of reality and illusion. It is an art form that was created to conform to certain real criteria—the stage, the distance, the lights, the stylized body language that conveys the dancers' message. But the criteria are, in a certain sense, also illusory, since they place a premium on making the unnatural appear natural, on forcing the dancer to transcend the laws of nature and, more generally, on creating a new series of aesthetic values. The apparent effortless quality of ballet is indeed an illusion, as my Florentine discovered as he stood in the wings, but this illusion is, after all, the reality of ballet.

*   *   *

The highly concentrated nature of ballet tends to turn most dancers into very nervous people. It is almost constitutionally impossible to be calm and relaxed when the successes or failures in your career depend on a few minutes of intense dancing, and when your artistry is constantly put to the test. A dancer's fame is ephemeral, and leaves no lasting mark, except in the specta- tor's memory. A dancer's fame is fluid, because it depends on the sum total of his or her performances, never on a single perfect moment. Finally, a dancer's fame is intangible, because it reflects a highly personal, yet harmonious, unity of movement, technique, maturity, musicality and "soul."

The anticipation of the performance builds up inner tension, and trans- forms some dancers into snappy "beasts" who irritate (if they are simple corps members) or terrorize (if they are great stars) the rest of the company. But show business would not be complete without temper tantrums. Dancers quickly develop a hard outer crust, and pay relatively little attention to their colleagues' "prima donna" behavior. Sometimes, however, the tension builds up to the explosion point. Then the ballerina will storm out of dress rehearsal because her partner does not support her properly in the difficult adagio sequence or is just a trifle slow in catching her in a fish. The soloist will scream at the corps girl who stepped in front of her. The senior corps member will snap at the novice who raised the wrong arm in the finale. And in this chaos the ballet mistress has to maintain quality and order, as well as her own sanity.

Despite all the backstage tension, there is a sense of excitement in the air. Even the routine preparations seem less tedious because of the anticipation of the performance. "A dancer is not human if she does not become nervous before a show," confesses Teena. "After all these years, I still get butterflies. When the stage loses its magic, then you know you're finished!"

There are different degrees of nervousness. When a dancer is scheduled for a routine part that she has done for years, the pre-performance flutters are minimal, and reflect the general sense of anticipation. When, however, she is doing a difficult ballet, the challenge justifies her acute case of butterflies. If she is doing an important new role, her colleagues share her case of nerves. Nobody would be gauche enough to wish her good luck. Theatrical etiquette requires one always to say the opposite of what one wants to say. Therefore, "Break a leg" means "Have a great performance!"

In the New York City Ballet, the most commonly used phrase for these occasions is the French five-letter word *merde*. Before curtain call, one dancer will remind another to "wish So-and-so *merde* because she is doing her first *Swan Lake.*" Because of such frequent use, the term has acquired a second meaning. It also refers to the special "good luck" gift, accompanied by a tiny slip of paper which reads: *"Merde!* Love, Teena."

Many dancers have their own private rituals before performance. Teena, for example, will never go on stage without her Indian ring—a gold $2.50 piece in an elegantly raised gold setting. This attractive coin ring is very unusual because the Indian head has been outlined in different colors of transparent enamels. About ten years ago, Pierluigi Masi, a well-known Florentine jeweler, gave Teena the ring as a gift. Since then, she has never danced without it. "It may sound silly, but I always touch my Indian before I go out on stage," admits Teena with an almost apologetic tone in her voice. But for really special occasions, she expects, and even requests, the special good luck kick you know where! If all this sounds silly and irrational, just think about the number of people who refuse to walk under ladders or who blanch when a black cat crosses their path. Despite the world's technological progress, superstitions still lurk in our subconsciousness.

* * *

Right before curtain call, the dancers practice a few last-minute steps. They are probably still wearing their leg warmers and maybe even a stole over their shoulders. Occasionally a dancer forgets to remove her woolies and dashes out on stage in baggy green leg warmers or an old sweater. Invariably the effect is humorous. The audience chuckles with amusement, especially when the "offender" finally realizes her oversight.

Many dancers like to place a trayful of essential equipment in a convenient backstage corner. This could include a mirror for quick hair and make-up adjustments, some talcum powder to absorb the perspiration and reduce that unattractive "wet" look, an assortment of hairpins and safety pins for emergencies, a glass of water to wet the backs of the toe shoes, and possibly a jar of honey for quick energy. Backstage there is always a handy bottle of smelling salts for emergencies, and somebody with a needle in hand to repair broken shoulder straps or torn toe shoe ribbons.

A careful dancer, having analyzed the idiosyncrasies of the various conductors, will check who is conducting the evening's performance. One conductor may like to speed up the tempos, even in the adagio sequence, where the ballerina likes to have plenty of time to show off her extension. Another may conduct the allegro sections at an exasperatingly slow pace, so that the dancer has to strain in the jumps. A good ballet conductor will watch the dancers, especially the principals, and will try to adjust the tempo in emergency situations. Nothing is more disturbing than seeing a dancer fly through the air on a downbeat, or end a pirouette at the beginning of a new phrase.

On tour, a ballet company takes along its own conductors, but never its own orchestra because of the tremendous expense that would involve. This means that the synchronization of music to the dancing becomes more challenging. The conductor has to "break in" a new orchestra in each new theater. Sometimes major problems arise if the orchestra has not been accustomed to playing for ballet, and the musicians are unwilling to adjust tempos to suit the dancers. The authenticity of the musical score cannot be compromised, they argue, and the dancers will simply have to move a little faster or a little more slowly. So the poor conductor is caught between two clashing groups of artists, and risks mutiny from an irate orchestra and a protest demonstration from the incensed dancers.

For small concert performances, the most frequent solution is taped music, which reduces the costs and eliminates the difficulties of working with a semi-amateur orchestra. While taped music may reduce the excitement of a live performance, it is less objectionable and more dependable than a shoddy orchestra.

There is always lots of talking backstage, and as we have seen, the dancers often talk on stage. Sometimes they call out cues to an understudy, other times they hiss out warnings to someone who has made a noticeable mistake. A ballerina may grunt, "Hold me," to her partner if she begins to fall off pointe, or "Not so tight" if he is squeezing her waist. A partner may occasionally whisper an encouraging word of praise after a particularly exacting sequence. Four-letter words often fly across the stage, when a dancer loses her balance, or "flubs" her turns. If the talking gets out of hand, the stage manager or his assistant will give a threatening order for immediate silence.

But the dancers are not the only people who talk. The stage crew talks, the ballet mistress talks, the wardrobe assistants talk. The wings are usually filled with people—dancers and occasionally dancers' friends—who watch the performers with cold, analytical eyes and criticize mistakes without an ounce of pity. The dancer on stage knows that she is being watched by the audience, but the audience, being an amorphous, homogeneous mass, seems less hostile than the familiar faces in the wings. But the dancer quickly learns that unless she blocks out the people in the wings, the quality of her dancing will suffer.

Lots of little, unexpected incidents can disturb the smooth running of a performance. Some are so minor that they are hardly worth mentioning. For example, a dancer may lose hairpins or earrings. The audience rarely notices these losses, unless somebody happens to trip on a stray earring or to slide on a bobby pin. While a dancer cannot look down to check the floor, she should occasionally glance around to see if there are any dangerous objects on the stage. If a dancer spots a potential danger, she will try to kick it inconspicuously into the wings. But this is not always possible.

Sometimes the audience is aware of these incidents. During a *Nutcracker* performance, one of the whirling Flowers lost her elegant headpiece, which landed right in the middle of the stage. The audience watched with concern as the dancers waltzed nervously around the obstacle. Finally Teena picked up the distracting headpiece with gallant aplomb and threw it into the wings. The audience cheered her slightly unorthodox solution with a resounding bravo, and then they settled back to enjoy the rest of the dancing.

On stage dancers sometimes lose part of their costumes. During a performance of *Western Symphony,* the ruffle on one of the ballerina's skirts became loose. When she started the series of rapid pirouettes in the finale, the force of the turns caused the stitching to unravel. As the poor Western ballerina spun around faster and faster, she became so entangled in the yards of ruffles that she had to run into the wings. After the offending ruffles had been quickly amputated by a be-scissored assistant, the ballerina dashed back on stage.

Not all costume accidents are humorous. Some bodices are cut so low that the ballerina's bosom may slip out when she does a deep lunge or an arched cambré. If her bust is generous, it may not slip back into her scanty costume. It is embarrassing to continue dancing in a "topless" tutu, while the backstage audience makes salacious comments. On a few rare occasions, both elastic straps have snapped, and left the startled ballerina nude from the waist up. Here the only solution is a quick exit and an even quicker repair job!

*   *   *

Mistakes are part of every dancer's career. Mistakes can be divided into two basic categories—the good ones, which the audience (and possibly the ballet mistress) does not notice, and the bad ones, which everyone sees. Nobody really remembers the good mistakes, because there are no immediate consequences, but everyone remembers the bad ones, because they really count.

The most common mistakes involve moving in the wrong direction. These errors often end in collisions. While they are rarely serious, they certainly break the magical spell of the ballet. More serious mistakes, especially in partnering work, occur if a dancer forgets a cue. In the *Stars and Stripes* pas de deux, the ballerina does a series of rapid turns and is caught in a spectacular arabesque by her partner, who dashes out of the wings at the very last moment. One performance, however, almost ended in disaster. The Liberty Bell ballerina, never doubting the good will of her partner, lunged into a great arabesque after the turns. Her partner never arrived, and the poor Bell crashed to the floor. The performance stopped until she recovered from the shock. By sheer will power, she finished the pas de deux, and received a standing ovation. But as soon as the curtain had dropped, the guilty partner received a violent tongue-lashing as well as a warning from the office.

There is an old ballet saying that you're not a real dancer until you've fallen on stage. Teena became a real dancer at the Bolshoi Theater. It was opening night for the New York City Ballet's first performance in the Soviet Union, Mr. Balanchine's first trip back to Russia since 1924—a history-making occasion for the American dancers and the enthusiastic Russian audience. Teena was dancing a corps de ballet part in the fourth movement of *Symphony in C*. She slipped in her first jump and fell flat on the stage in a perfect spread-eagle. The impact of the fall was so great that she lay stunned in that ignominious position for several seconds. "I was mortified," she recalls. "Of all places to fall—the Bolshoi on opening night. If the old saying is true, then I really made it in a great way in a great place!" But sometimes one has the feeling that this old saying never really compensates for the humiliation of falling on stage.

Sometimes a dancer falls because somebody else has made a mistake: another dancer may trip or bump her; her partner may err in calculating a jump or lift. One of the most spectacular falls that Teena remembers happened in *Scotch Symphony*. At one point, two tartan-clad boys raise the lovely Sylph and literally throw her across the stage to her Scottish prince, who is supposed to catch his love. One evening, however, the two boys threw the Sylph with such force that the prince actually fell over backward as he caught her. The misty, romantic spell of love was shattered as the Sylph and her love tumbled to the floor. Fortunately neither was hurt. After a moment of surprise, they finished the adagio.

Other accidents on stage could be termed technical. A dancer gets caught on a piece of scenery or on a prop, and has to struggle to get free. There may be mechanical difficulties, such as the Christmas tree in *The Nutcracker* that jams and does not grow, as it is supposed to do. Or the curtain may get stuck halfway. Then the poor dancers have to hold their final pose until it is completely lowered. There are mistakes with the lighting—too much, too little, wrong colors, no spotlights on the ballerina. But these technical accidents have occurred ever since the birth of ballet. Today safety precautions on stage have to meet high standards. Less than a century ago, however, the stage was a dangerous firetrap because it was lit with gas lamps. One promising young ballerina had her career brought to a tragic end when her skirt caught on fire. The poor girl died shortly afterward from her burns.

* * *

On tour, there are many reasons why performing becomes more difficult. First of all, it is tiring to move from one city to another, with the added nuisance of double packing—clothes and personal effects as well as a theater case. It is frustrating to be tied down by a rigid rehearsal and performance schedule, and have no time for sightseeing and shopping. Finally, it is physically and psychologically exhausting to have to get used to new stages and new orchestras. A dancer, like most human beings, is also a creature of habit who feels comfortably safe on a familiar stage.

One of the greatest fears that plague a dancer is a poor stage, which can compromise the success of a performance. A stage is poor if it is small and shallow, if the wings are narrow, if the lighting is inadequate. A dancer usually includes cold and drafty conditions among the characteristics of a poor stage, because the risk of cramped muscles is greater.

In Europe, some stages are raked—that is, perpendicularly sloped toward the audience. The raked stage is especially suited to opera, because the audience can see all the singers, even those in the back. American dancers, however, are used to performing on a level stage, and are disoriented when they have to switch to a raked one. They frequently lose their balance, because the floor slopes forward under their feet. They have to remember that jumps are only done downstage—that is, toward the audience. As long as they jump downstage, the tilt of the floor creates the optical illusion of greater elevation. If they forget and jump upstage, they look like heavy, straining amateurs who need a few more years of good, serious training.

It takes a while for the dancer to adjust to the sloped floor. Sometimes sections of a ballet have to be rechoreographed. Many years ago, when the New York City Ballet was dancing in Portugal, several highly technical ballets had to be canceled because the stage was so severely raked. Quite literally, the dancers nearly slipped into the orchestra pit!

Teena recalls her first experience with a raked stage. It was in Russia at the Bolshoi Theater, the night of her spread-eagle fall in *Symphony in C*. The ballet company alternated performances between the famous Bolshoi and the modern Kremlin Theater. The wardrobe mistress hated this complex schedule, because she had to have the costumes moved between the two theaters. The stage manager and his assistants hated it because they had to remember all the technical differences between the two theaters. But most of all, the dancers hated it. In addition to carting shoes, make-up and other vital ballet accessories between the two theaters, they had to dance one evening on the raked stage at the Bolshoi and another on the level stage at the Kremlin. "It nearly drove us out of our minds," Teena says, laughing now. "At the end of a pirouette or a jump, nobody could remember whether to land normally or to hold up one's back and compensate for the tilt of the raked stage. It was wild!"

The surface of the stage is another important feature. A rough, lumpy wooden stage with cracks between the boards can cause the dancers to fall. The New York City Ballet has all but eliminated this problem. At Lincoln Center, the stage is always covered with a linoleum "floor" which reduces the problems of slipping, noise (especially the toe shoe "clunk") and uneven surfaces. On tour, the company always carries this linoleum floor (and an extra one for emergencies) in order to keep the injury rate at a minimum.

While the linoleum practically eliminates all the surface problems, it cannot soften a hard stage—a cement floor covered with wood. The wooden covering gives as the dancers jump, but the cement does not; therefore, the impact of this hard landing tires and cramps the leg muscles. If you want to have an idea of what a hard stage feels like, just start practicing a few assemblés or grands jetés on the nearest sidewalk!

For guest performances, a dancer obviously cannot carry her own floor. If she is dancing for a large company, the stage is usually, though not always, good. If, however, she is scheduled for a concert performance in a small town, the stage may be "death," as Teena would define it. For these occasions, some ballerinas use rubber-tipped and -soled toe shoes, which reduce the risks of slipping. The rubber makes the shoes heavier, but better a heavy toe than a possible fall!

Atmospheric conditions can make touring unpleasant, especially if the performances are presented in open-air theaters. In Athens, the New York City Ballet danced in the historic Herodes Atticus Theater at the foot of the Acropolis. The outdoor theater was a perfect setting for the evening performances, but a veritable inferno under the white August sun. Before opening night, there was a late afternoon dress rehearsal on stage. Despite the late hour, the sun was still so strong that several dancers fainted. Worst of all, the linoleum floor began to melt! After that experience, no rehearsals were scheduled in the theater. The linoleum was neatly rolled up and placed in a safe, cool spot each night after the performance.

In Dubrovnik, the dancers had to cope once again with the intense Mediterranean heat. Classes and rehearsals were scheduled at a nearby ballet school, never at the outdoor theater, which was located on top of the old fort. One evening, the wind was so strong that it almost threatened to blow away the town. Though the performance was not canceled, all the scenery, props, backdrops, wings and curtain had to be removed as a safety precaution. The

Talking to fans after the performance

performance was almost eerie in this skeleton setting. The wind played havoc with the soft ballerina-length skirts. Occasionally a girl got caught in the vortex of her costume. The wind made it difficult for the corps to stand still, and actually blew some dancers off balance. "The worst thing was the dust," recalls Teena. "I was terrified of getting something under my contact lenses. Fortunately I was wearing a new pair of super-long lashes, which flapped in the wind but saved my eyes from the dust!"

Another annoying aspect of night performances in outdoor theaters is the bug problem. At Saratoga, the summer home of the New York City Ballet, the dancers are devoured by the mosquitoes attracted by the lights. "There are bugs all over the place," complains Teena, "and they fly into your mouth, ears and eyes as you dance. They bite too, but you can't stop dancing to scratch a mosquito bite."

Open-air performances are sometimes interrupted by violent rainstorms, which drench dancers and audience alike. To minimize such atmospheric risks, many of the new outdoor theaters are built with an overhead roof but no walls. This makes it possible for the dancers to practice during the day without collapsing from sunstroke, but actually the roof is of little help in a lashing rain. Once, Teena recalls, the music suddenly stopped because the orchestra pit was flooded. The musicians all ran out, carrying their precious instruments, as the dancers and audience watched in amazement.

Outdoor theaters can be cold, damp and even muddy, if the weather is bad. The dancers bundle themselves up with extra sweaters and leg warmers, and shiver when they have to strip down to the pure costume and step out on stage. The strong spotlights are not powerful enough to counteract the drafts and the damp night air. Many dancers catch nasty summer colds during these tours.

Teena maintains that the worst outdoor experience was in Columbia, Maryland. The theater was only partially completed by opening night, and the customary backstage amenities did not even exist. The dancers used trailers as makeshift dressing rooms, and picked their way to the stage on a crude path of uneven, wobbly boards. "It was dangerous walking in toe shoes, because one wrong step and you could twist an ankle." The situation became almost surrealistic after a particularly heavy rainstorm, which turned the backstage area into a muddy lake. The dancers were trapped in their trailers. They could not be expected to walk through the mud in tights and ballet slippers, and then get out on stage and dance, so the stagehands had to carry them back and forth.

* * *

When the curtain comes down, the dancers quickly take their places for the bows. This is probably the most emotionally packed moment of the entire show. The exhausted ballerina is happy that the challenge is over, and is radiant if the audience applauds her performance. She smiles graciously as she receives the long-stemmed red roses sent by an infatuated admirer. The corps de ballet girls watch jealously and dream about the day when they too will be bowing in front of a cheering audience. Yet all the dancers experience a pang of sadness as they walk off stage. The show is over. Though their feet are sore and their bodies are tired, they instinctively long for the glamorous excitement of the performance, and unconsciously resent the return to routine reality.

It never ceases to amaze me how quickly the dancers, musicians and stage crew leave the theater after the show. In a matter of minutes, the stage is deserted and lifeless. There is no more excitement, no more vitality, just a great big silent void. "Everyone burns out," explains Teena, "because the stage is alive before and during a performance. Afterwards it is dead and so, so sad."

Chapter 11

A Dancer's Typical Nonschedule

A dancer's body resembles a superb precision instrument, with one important difference. The precision is acquired, not innate. The human body was not created for ballet, and therefore it must be trained before it achieves the necessary coordination and muscle control. The first commandment in every dancer's life is never to forget the daily routine. Instant ballet just does not exist. Nine hours of practice in one day does not yield the same results as nine hours distributed over three days in separate three-hour sessions. Every dancer knows that her muscles need the proper dose of daily exercise (the exact amount, of course, varies from individual to individual), but rebel when overworked.

In a certain sense, the regularity of the ballet schedule makes the dancer a slave to her daily routine. She has to practice, or must suffer the consequences —immediate consequences, which include sore, stiff muscles or faltering balance, and long-range ones, which eventually destroy her technique. This rigid regularity conditions her personal freedom of choice. Before she takes a complete ten-day vacation, she has to weigh her decision carefully. Undoubtedly the rest will do her body and her soul a lot of good. Her overworked muscles will shrink and lose that unattractive knottiness. By the end of a long, hard season, Teena admits that she has difficulty wearing some of her shoes and boots, because her feet and legs are swollen from the strain of so much dancing. "But after a week or so of total rest," she adds, "the uncomfortable shoes fit perfectly, and the comfortable pairs are even loose."

While the body is refreshed by a complete rest, the muscles lose some of their elasticity and become stiff. It takes anywhere from ten days to two weeks to "get back into shape" after a short vacation. The rest is well worth the aches and pains unless the dancer has important engagements. In these cases, she cannot afford "muscularly" to take the rest because she would not be in shape for her guest star appearance or her TV engagement. Between seasons, the dancers usually have two to three weeks free. These layoff periods are the ideal time for a vacation. Everybody in the company needs the rest, and everybody—dancers, ballet mistress and choreographer—knows that most of the dancers will be stiff and sore during the first week of rehearsals.

* * *

The glitter and glamour of the performance cause most people to forget the demanding nature of a dancer's life. When Teena's friends learn about her routine, they wonder how she can stand the daily classes, the long hours of rehearsal, the weeks of performing and the complete dedication to her work. "Why, you don't have a moment to yourself during the season!" they exclaim with sincere amazement. "How can you stand it? It sounds inhuman." Six days of work, with Monday as the free day; eight performances a week, with matinee and evening performances on both Saturdays and Sundays; as many as eight hours of rehearsal, scheduled anywhere between 11 A.M. and 11 P.M.—thus the dancer's day is fragmented. Even when she is not actually dancing, she is probably waiting in the theater for her next rehearsal. Since rehearsal schedules are posted daily, not weekly, it is practically impossible to make plans for the week. Furthermore, schedules in the ballet world are subject to last-minute changes, for valid—and sometimes not so valid—reasons. The dancer is always on call.

The situation is even more demanding during the season. Though the casting for the performances is posted weekly, it too is subject to change. Sometimes a dancer injures herself, and a particular ballet has to be canceled. By law, every dancer, whether or not she is scheduled to perform, must check in every evening by one-half hour before curtain call, or risk a fine and a severe reprimand. If she does not report in personally at the theater, she must phone

to see whether she is needed, and in an emergency, must race over to the theater and replace a dancer who cannot perform. These last-minute "fill-ins," a constant source of worry to the corps de ballet members, are less frequent frustrations for the soloists and the principals, except perhaps at the end of a long season or on tour.

A dancer's time is never really her own except during the layoff. Her schedule is always subject to revision, and she must be available. She can really count on only twelve hours of privacy each day. According to union law, at least twelve hours must elapse between the end of a performance and the beginning of the first rehearsal. Therefore, if the performance ends at 11:08 P.M., the first rehearsal cannot be scheduled earlier than 11:08 the following morning.

This rigid schedule would certainly be inhuman to anyone except a dancer, and at times it becomes unbearable even to her. A dancer, however, has been used to this regimented life ever since the early days of her training. Studying ballet represents a considerable investment of time. Since serious ballet training in the United States is not part of the school curriculum, the child must attend a specialized ballet school after regular academic hours. If she has professional aspirations, she must take at least six classes a week. Adding the actual length of the lesson to the time spent in transportation, taking ballet means fitting up to three hours of dance into the busy daily schedule of a high school student. It also implies that the ballet student has to give up some of the more conventional extracurricular activities.

Most secondary schools today are willing to accommodate, within reasonable limits, students who want to pursue professional ballet training. When I was studying, however, Mother had to beg the principal for special permission so that I could be excused twenty minutes early from a last-period study hall! Worst of all, Mother's request was considered vaguely immoral, since she was encouraging her nice suburban daughter to associate with the highly questionable New York ballet world.

Exposure to the demanding ballet schedule is not enough to make one grow accustomed to all the sacrifices. A ballerina does not merely like her work. She loves it, otherwise she would quit. She lives ballet, she breathes it, she feels it, she dreams it, and sometimes she even hates it. But love and hate, as everyone knows, are really two sides of the same coin.

Ballet is much more than a full-time job. Ballet is a way of life. It is a closed, autonomous world with its own special rules, its own special values and its own special problems. It is possible for a dancer to live inside this ballet bubble and be completely impervious to the joys and crises of the outside world. In a certain sense, this existence parallels the ivory tower syndrome of academia, with the same isolation, the same self-perpetuating ideals and the same inbred interests.

The autonomy of the ballet world is a mixed blessing for the dancer. On the one hand, it allows her to concentrate on her dancing with a minimum of outside distractions. As long as she remains within this familiar world, she will be surrounded by people, things and situations that exude ballet. On the other hand, this special ballet world can grow monotonous because of the lack of external stimuli.

Some dancers feel the urge for variety. They want to meet new people who are not dancers, discover new interests that are not necessarily connected with ballet, discuss new ideas that do not concern dance. "I like to step out of my world every once in a while," explains Teena, "so I don't lose my sense of perspective."

Teena also maintains that her outside interests have helped her mature both as an individual and as a dancer. During a long layoff, she likes to travel. She has traveled all over the world. "I love to go to new places and meet new people. Traveling makes you see so many different sides of life—good and bad, beautiful and ugly, stimulating and depressing. But perhaps most of all, traveling makes you realize that most things in life are relative, not absolute."

Many people envy dancers when they go on tour. Touring can be exciting, but it can also be a tiring routine of new theaters, new orchestras, new hotels and very little free time. On tour, the dancers have the same six-day schedule, with one important difference. The travel day cannot coincide with the free day, except in very special cases when the dancers are paid overtime—but overtime is not the same as free time. In addition to the inconveniences of hotel living, the dancers have to cope with the strange, unfamiliar schedules of foreign countries. In many cities, eating becomes a major problem. The food is new, and perhaps unsuited to the dancer's special eating habits. The meal hours are often set, with no allowance made for anyone who, even for a very valid reason, cannot dine then. Sometimes these minor inconveniences can assume the proportions of major nuisances. But for the dancer, as indeed for the average tourist, they are an inevitable part of traveling abroad.

*   *   *

Like all precision instruments, a dancer's body should receive special care. In theory, a dancer should follow a very regular schedule and get plenty of sleep. She gets exercise in her work, of course, but must be careful not to overindulge even in good, healthy food, unless she wants to risk losing her job. Overweight dancers are suspended if they are lucky, and fired—or to use a current euphemism, "let go"—if they are unlucky. Because of the tremendous physical exertion, sleep becomes a pressing physiological need. "You just cannot dance," cautions Teena, "if you're dead tired. The body rebels, and that's that, unless you resort to artificial stimuli. But they can be *very* dangerous."

A dancer must take good care of her body. Some care is therapeutic—carefully disinfecting open blisters, massaging cramped muscles, exercising weak or injured tendons. Some care is preventive—protecting a blister with a soft foam pad, strapping an old strain to minimize the risks of a relapse, or keeping a weak tendon warm.

Special attention must be given to the feet, which are probably the dancer's single most important instrument. She should wear good shoes that give her "precious" feet the correct support. Sometimes she must sacrifice fashion for comfort. Most dancers avoid wearing the high platform sandals for fear of twisting an ankle, or shoes with narrow, pointed toes for fear of irritating old corns or developing new ones.

Because of the strain of toe dancing, the muscles in a dancer's foot are often overdeveloped, the bones in the toes are gnarled and the arch may be abnormally high. As a result, she often has difficulty in finding comfortable shoes. Teena will wear only Italian shoes—not any kind of Italian shoes, but Mantellassi shoes, which are sold only in Florence and Bologna. This means that Teena buys shoes when she comes to visit me in Florence, or appropriates my shoes—since we wear the same size—when I come back to New Jersey for a visit. She maintains that my shoes feel better because I break them in perfectly. "After all, Joanie, it's so easy for *you* to buy shoes," she purrs winsomely. "You can get another pair when you get back to Florence." Needless to say, the cost of keeping my sister in comfortable shoes plays havoc with my shoe bill, but it is for a "sacred" cause—the protection of a ballerina's feet!

*   *   *

A dancer must spend a lot of time on body maintenance. While a moderate dose of daily exercise improves the general health, the strain of ballet drains the body's reserve supplies. If a dancer abuses her body, her entire system will be weakened. Therefore, she must take good care of her body.

Aside from the close attention given to feet, muscles and tendons, a dancer must take special care of her skin. She perspires profusely, she rolls all over the floor, she practices adagio work with boys who also perspire profusely. The studios and the stages are sometimes dirty and are certainly dusty from the rosin the dancers use. Unless she washes herself and her practice clothes thoroughly and frequently, she will probably develop skin rashes.

"Creaming off your make-up after performance is a real torture," sighs Teena. "When you're exhausted, who feels like taking ten minutes to get your face and neck really clean?" Because of the frequent touch-ups, the make-up works its way deep into the pores, so most girls cream their face thoroughly two or three times.

Sometimes the girls are lazy. They rub a dot of cold cream into their face, whisk it off with one tissue and splash a few drops of soapy water over their face. Other times they are sloppy. Instead of putting on fresh make-up, they repair their faces with a thick layer of powder and race out for an after-performance date. A dancer has to get ready quickly because her friends usually do not want to wait half an hour while she "primps." Perhaps they do not even understand why she needs so much time to get dressed.

Unfortunately some dancers develop poor pimply complexions because they do not practice meticulous skin care. Teena maintains that the best way to remove the deep traces of make-up and perspiration is first to cream the face thoroughly and then to rub it with cotton pads soaked in alcohol. Most cosmeticians would probably consider Teena's solution highly unorthodox and even dangerous, because alcohol dries out the skin. "Of course alcohol dries out the skin," retorts Teena, "but it also happens to be the best way for a dancer to deep-clean her pores. Afterwards you have to use lots of moisturizers. The alternative is dirty, oily skin."

Oils and emollient lotions are the secret to smooth, supple skin. Since Teena takes two to three baths or showers a day, she always uses bath oil in the water: "Otherwise I'd probably shed my skin like an old snake." She rubs her feet every night with a medicated moisturizing cream called Dermassage to minimize the risks of fungus and to keep the skin on her toes from cracking. "The combination of perspiration, nylon tights and toe dancing really makes your feet burn," she explains. She often rubs her entire body with afterbath creams to keep the skin soft. "The spotlights dry out the skin, and you have to lubricate yourself." Teena becomes highly incensed when some of her friends accuse her of being sybaritic in her body-maintenance routine. "You get only one body," she snaps, "and it's your duty to keep it in tiptop condition. It should run well, and look good." And to prove her point, she begins citing examples of how body maintenance was almost a sacred duty to the ancient Egyptians, the Greeks, the Romans, and so forth.

Some dancers have weak, thin hair because they tie it back in a tight bun or a French twist. Add to that lots of perspiration, heavy headpieces which have to be securely anchored with scores of hairpins, hair spray to keep short loose ends in place, and strong spotlights which quite literally burn the hair. The final result is thin, lusterless hair that demands special care—natural shampoos with no detergent agents, oil conditioners and lots of proper brushing with a good brush.

Important as these specific points of body maintenance are, they will not produce miracles if a dancer is overtired and undernourished. Plenty of sleep restores much of the body's energies, but sleep alone is not enough if the body's reserve supplies are depleted. A proper diet is perhaps the single most important factor in body maintenance. There are many theories as to what constitutes a proper diet, and perhaps even more answers. Dancers, on the whole, tend to follow the newest diet craze, especially the ones that are "thin-oriented." Certainly the constant preoccupation of all dancers, especially the girls, is how to stay thin. Overweight is almost a sin in the ballet world, for two important reasons. First of all, it is more difficult to dance when one is heavy because there is more weight to move, lift and balance. Secondly, the strong spotlights play cruel tricks, and add unwanted pounds in unwanted places!

Maintaining a svelte figure can represent a considerable sacrifice to anyone with a hearty appetite or a slow metabolism. Unfortunately, the best way to lose weight is to reduce one's intake of calories, and the best way to stay thin is to watch one's diet. There are really no miracle ways to lose weight. Weight loss or weight control can sometimes be more difficult for a dancer than for a "normal" person. Since a dancer moves more, she may have a bigger appetite. Her muscles are more developed, and therefore even the smallest layer of fat will make her appear heavier. Dieting means reducing one's supplies of energy, which in turn makes dancing more tiring.

Some lucky dancers do not have a weight problem. They simply have to take care not to overeat or overindulge in highly fattening foods or alcohol. Others have to deprive themselves of most of the "joys of eating" if they want to remain thin. At times they rebel against this rigid diet, and go on a sinfully sensuous "eating binge." The penance is a starvation diet, seasoned with guilt about their newly acquired fatty bulges.

Because of the physical strain of ballet and the constant worry about weight gain, dancers are always looking for high-energy, low-calorie foods. Some girls nibble sesame or sunflower seeds between rehearsals, others take a few spoonfuls of pure honey before performance. Most girls prefer diet sodas, which really cut down the calories and at the same time quench their thirst. "We get so dehydrated on stage from perspiring and from the lights that we have to drink a lot," explains Teena. "But too much regular soda is a disaster for the figure and for the teeth. That's why I've learned to like diet soda."

Many dancers supplement their diet with a hearty supply of daily vitamins. Teena takes at least seven vitamins a day, and maintains that they keep her strong and healthy. "Lots of people—and I won't mention names—mock my vitamin theory, but I'm rarely sick, and have more energy than most of them." Despite pressure and persuasion to the contrary, Teena really believes in her vitamin ritual.

*　　*　　*

One of the most frequent questions people ask Teena is to describe a typical day in a ballerina's life. They want to know when she gets up, what she eats and how she spends her time. Teena muses thoughtfully before answering: "There is really no such thing as a typical day in a ballerina's life." Quite literally, a dancer lives from day to day. Unlike most "normal" jobs, ballet does not have a fixed nine-to-five schedule. The dancer has three basic kinds of schedule: the performance schedule, the rehearsal schedule and the layoff periods, when she may rest, take class or do guest performances. But within these three basic divisions, her schedule varies from one day to the next. She can never be sure of what she will have to do the following day. "The uncertainty is probably one of the hardest things to get used to. Your daily schedule is always subject to last-minute changes."

This "nonschedule," however, presupposes an availability that is not required by most other jobs. "If you don't love your work," cautions Teena, "you quickly grow to resent all the intrusions in your personal life." A dancer must be willing to make many sacrifices for her art. Her social life is limited because of her rehearsal and performance schedule. She can never be sure, until the last minute, whether she will be able to go to that Saturday night party or whether she will be free for New Year's Eve. She may be expected to dance at the last minute.

Dancers have the reputation of being exotic individuals who transcend the banalities of daily existence. Men often find ballerinas irresistible. After the initial fascination has passed, though, many get tired of the usual answer: "I'd love to go *if* I'm not dancing." They have difficulty in understanding, perhaps even more difficulty in accepting, the nonschedule in a ballerina's life. And while they cannot criticize her for not planning ahead, they vent their impotent wrath on what they describe as the inefficient ballet organization. What these outside critics forget, however, is that the ballet world does not follow the rules and schedules of the business world. Ballet (and show business in general) is a world unto itself.

A dancer's motto must be "Ballet first and then all the rest." If she is single, this means working her private life, as best she can, around her ballet schedule. Many girls prefer dating fellow dancers, because in this way they eliminate the problems and tensions of trying to combine a dancer's schedule with a nondancer's. Two dancers have the same goals, the same problems and the same nonschedule. Above all, they share the same preoccupation with their art. "The only trouble with marrying a dancer," reasons Teena, "is that you never get out of the ballet world. It's fine for some people, but for others, like me, it wouldn't work. I'd feel too restricted."

When a dancer is married to a nondancer—and these marriages do occur —her partner must be willing to accept all the consequences, positive and negative, of having a dancer as a wife. She will spend little time at home, will often be away on tour, and will not always be free in the evening. She will be the exotic artist, and he may sometimes feel like a forgotten member of the family. If there are children, the daily routine becomes even more complicated.

These are just a few of the reasons why some dancers do not marry, or marry later on in life. "Our schedule is incompatible with most other people's," explains Teena, "and most other people don't want to put up with our wild, crazy, yet wonderful world." But perhaps this incompatible schedule is not the only reason why some dancers do not worry about marriage. In a certain sense, they are already married to their art. Because being a ballerina means being in love with ballet and being willing to forget about all the rest. I know that this is really the basic difference between Teena and me. I danced and gave it up, because I only liked ballet. Teena is still dancing, because she adores it.

Chapter 12

Why Ballet?

Being a ballet dancer means many different things. It takes long years of arduous training to master the muscle control, grace and harmony required, as well as constant daily practice to keep the muscles in perfect working condition. It implies living according to a demanding schedule that leaves little time for outside interests. It means being one hundred percent body conscious, and as a result, one hundred percent conditioned by one's body.

Along with the dancer's unromantic daily routine—but every activity has its dreary side—there are moments of supreme recognition which more than compensate her for her efforts and her sacrifices. The stage offers the dancer a unique occasion to express herself through her art. All her efforts are directed toward those few moments during which she makes the audience experience love, pity, anger, fear or simply a vision of pure beauty. The spectator forgets his own identity, and is magnetically drawn into her world of dance, where he participates at the visual and emotional level.

The performance is the central moment in a dancer's life. She spends a lot of time preparing for it, and afterward a lot of time thinking about it. That good "after the show" glow quickly fades. The dancer always hopes that her next performance will be better. She strives for greater perfection.

A dancer is content to live on her laurels only when she has retired. Then the active part of her career has ended. Either she forgets dance completely or she devotes her ballet energies to teaching. Though most young, ambitious dancers define teaching as the consolation prize for old or unsuccessful dancers, many change their opinion when they stop performing. Perhaps some teach because they feel it is a more dignified way to accept retirement. Others do so because they discover that teaching can be a creative, rewarding experience even though it does not receive the direct recognition of performing. The performer is applauded for her own merits, while the teacher is applauded indirectly through the merits of her pupils.

When a dancer retires and starts to teach, her perspectives usually change dramatically. Maybe for the first time in her life, she realizes the importance of tradition. In her own small way, she is passing on her personal experience to young dancers, who will in turn do the same when they stop dancing. Perhaps only when time has worn off her highly competitive crust can she view her own career as part of the great ballet stream rather than as an isolated success story.

But does the glitter of the stage really make up for all the preparatory routine? It all depends on the individual. In the final analysis, every choice or decision in life is highly personal and subjective. The important thing is to be convinced of one's choice and to love what one has chosen to do. In this way, one can better weigh the successes, disappointments and failures that dot the careers of even the great stars.

*　*　*

Today dance and pop music are probably the two most vital art forms in the United States. In the last decade, there has been a veritable surge of interest in dance. New schools have sprung up, dance departments have been created in many colleges and universities, regional dance companies have been formed all over the country, not only in the sophisticated suburban areas around the large cities. While this new interest has involved all kinds of dance, ballet has perhaps made the greatest strides. We can really speak of a ballet boom.

Naturally, not all the manifestations of this new interest in ballet are positive. Some of the new schools are staffed with inadequately trained teachers, who will be unable to prepare their students for a professional career. Some of the regional companies lack good dancers and dynamic choreographers. Part of the enthusiasm for ballet is probably another example of the faddism that characterizes American life. Even so, this fad seems more serious than most, and in the last ten years has influenced American tastes, especially among the younger generation.

Perhaps the most important change involves the new status of dance. Today dance is no longer taboo, and the dancer is no longer a strange, peripheral member of society. Dancers, and artists in general, are respected individuals who make serious contributions to society. Sometimes they are even the pace setters. Being an artist often works in one's favor. Frequently Teena and I go to the same cocktail parties. We strike up the usual conversations: "What's your name?" "Where are you from?" "What do you do?" Almost invariably, my companion uses the conventionally polite excuse "I have to refresh my martini, but I'll be back in a second, love," as soon as he hears what I do. People at a cocktail party are afraid of a professor, especially if she is a Romance philologist. And two minutes later, I see my former companion return, martini in hand, to court Teena, the ballerina. Everybody at a cocktail party is fascinated by a dancer, especially if she is as pretty as Teena. As for me, I have learned never to tell people at parties what I do, unless I want to get rid of them.

Despite this surge of interest in ballet, teaching methods have not kept pace with the new vitality at the performing level. I certainly do not want to denigrate the methods that have been developed by excellent teachers in the past and that are still valid. But there is an important limitation in all ballet instruction in the United States: it presents ballet only at the technical level, and ignores the background, the traditions and even the physiological reasons for body placement. In other words, you study ballet in order to become a ballerina, not to learn about ballet as an art form. Especially in a serious ballet school, success is equated with joining a good ballet company, and failure is synonymous with "quitting," even if *you* decide to stop dancing.

While a serious, competitive atmosphere helps maintain high quality, the scope of American ballet instruction is often limited to technique. A girl may be an excellent dancer, and yet know practically nothing about the ballet tradition. Whether or not we like to admit it, tradition cannot be ignored, because it is part of our cultural formation. The future is determined by how each present generation reacts to the past. It does not really matter whether the particular reactions are positive or negative, because in either case, the past influences the present.

The same holds true for ballet, where the traditional influences still run strong despite the experimentalism of some iconoclastic choreographers. But many dancers have no concern for tradition, simply out of ignorance. Both Teena and I studied ballet at excellent schools, and learned how to dance correctly. But in ballet we used our bodies, and at school we used our minds. We instinctively separated the two activities, as many people continue to do even today. We never imagined that the two might be interrelated. It was not until we went to an unusual summer dance workshop in Maine, run by Albertine Maxwell, that we began to understand why dance was not a separate, peripheral activity in society. As we studied Hindu dance with Miss Dieman and Miss Bennett, two interesting ladies who had lived and studied in India, we realized that without an understanding of tradition, we could not really dance. Studying dance meant more than learning how to do certain steps; it also meant learning about that particular dance form.

Since we had classes in ballet, Hindu and Spanish dance, we had ample opportunity to compare the three forms, to discuss the basic similarities and differences, and best of all, to get to know the teachers. We heard wild stories about living in India, and funny experiences in Albertine's career as a Spanish dancer. But Teena and I most enjoyed the after-dinner chats with Felia Doubrovska and her husband, Pierre Vladimiroff, who had been Pavlova's partner from 1928 to 1931. They told us about the Maryinsky School, where they had trained, their performances before the czar, their dangerous escape from Russia in 1918, their initial difficulties in Paris and their ballet successes all over Europe. We realized that these two Russian dancers were proud to belong to the great flowing ballet tradition—a tradition that was flexible enough to accept change and yet conservative enough to respect the past.

Even today this sense of tradition lives on in Russia. The attempts by hardcore revolutionaries to condemn ballet as another example of czarist decadence failed because the love of ballet has always been deeply rooted in the Russian people. The Bolshoi Theater, founded by the Empress Catherine in 1776, has just celebrated its two hundredth anniversary. Today the old classical ballets are performed side by side with the new, socialist-inspired ones. To commemorate this event, Brezhnev awarded all the members of the Bolshoi Theater—from the dancers to the janitors—the Order of Lenin, for it was Lenin who saved this great theater from destruction.

Ballet in the U.S.S.R. is taught at state-run schools. Students are admitted —there are only sixty openings each year at the Bolshoi School—after a series of rigid examinations in which they are screened for good bodies, strong, agile muscles, excellent health and details such as delicate hands or long necks for the girls. The training lasts eight years, and upon graduation the students are guaranteed a position. During the training the schedule is severe: long hours of ballet classes along with academic courses, no smoking, no drinking. According to one of the older pupils, every detail in the young dancers' lives is organized by the school. When they are old enough to be interested in the other sex, they are permitted to have quiet, regular relationships that do not drain aspiring dancers' vital energies!

This regimented schedule would seem excessive to Americans, who prefer a more permissive system of education. Certainly the early age at which the Russian child must choose his or her future career would disturb most Americans. The aim of American education is to expose the student to new and different fields *before* he decides upon his career. Thus the emphasis of American education tends to be general, superficial and, at times, disconnected. In Europe and Russia, however, the student is required to select his career at an earlier age, and then to concentrate in depth on that particular area. The price for this early specialization is a lack of alternatives, which in the opinion of many Americans would constitute a restriction of freedom of choice.

With regard to ballet, the difference in the two systems illustrates why ballet training in the United States is considered a separate, isolated specialization. While the American approach permits the student greater freedom in choosing and developing other interests, it limits the depth of their ballet training. They learn only about today's classroom routine, today's performances and today's bright choreographers. But it is a shame that they know next to nothing about yesterday's classroom routine, yesterday's performances and yesterday's bright choreographers.

Tradition becomes even more important if we consider ballet a language. It is body language. Like all languages, its goal is communication. Like all languages, ballet changes in time and in space—that is, it has evolved throughout the years, and varies from place to place at any given moment. Since ballet is a living language, its present form is not its final form. As long as ballet lives, it will continue to change.

Many people look slightly askance when ballet is defined as a means of communication. They instinctively equate communication with words, and ignore any other possibilities. One does indeed communicate with written and spoken words, but they are not the only means.

Body language is a valid, vital form of communication which has a rich expressive potential. The images of ballet are visual, but they are usually reinforced by music. Thus the channels of communication are dual: the eyes and the ears. In one way, the body language of ballet may be a more modern means of communication than the more conventional verbal language. In this era of mass media, the new forms of communication tend to be visual. Just consider for a moment how the movies and especially television have changed people's habits. Yesterday people read the newspaper or listened to news on the radio; today most look at TV to see and hear the news.

There is, however, one inherent danger in this new form of audiovisual communication. The viewer-listener does not participate. Communication thus becomes a one-way road on which the information moves from the active performer to the passive viewer-listener. While it is pleasant to receive messages, perhaps it is too pleasant and too easy. Simply receiving means no work and no involvement. This may be one of the reasons why spectator sports and spectator arts are so popular. A lot of people just want to sit back and watch.

While ballet may, in one sense, be more modern than the conventional forms of verbal communication, it faces one drawback. Many people do not know how to "read" the language of ballet. They look, approve or disapprove, but rarely can explain their reaction. If they knew a little about the language of ballet, they would be able to understand what the dancers want to express through their movements.

During the various lecture demonstrations on ballet that Teena and I have given, we have always defined ballet as a language in which the entire body "speaks" to the audience. If the viewer familiarizes himself with the alphabet of ballet, he will be able to form words and sentences. Then he will be able to "read" and understand what he sees. It does not matter if he does not become an expert, because even a superficial reading is valid. Though few of the viewers will remember all the technical terminology in our lecture demonstrations, they begin to see how coordinated body movement can convey meaning. The messages in the story ballets, like *The Sleeping Beauty* or *The Prodigal Son,* are concrete. The ones in the pure dance ballets, like *Ballet Imperial* or *Movements for Piano and Orchestra,* are abstract; here the dancer becomes a visual extension of the music.

With a basic understanding of the language of ballet, the viewer is no longer relegated to the position of a passive spectator who simply receives audiovisual messages. He can participate indirectly and can judge the efficacy of the dancer's desire to communicate. And if the viewer has studied ballet, there is a secret, magnetic amalgamation between the dancer and the viewer. In both instances, the channels of communication are two-way, even though one party is seated in the audience and the other is performing on the stage.

*   *   *

Why choose ballet? Ballet is only one of the many forms of communication that exist today. It is neither better nor worse than any other. But like all means of communication, it commands respect, because the dancer stretches out of his or her own personal world to reach other people. The dancer wants to tell them something.

People often ask me why I gave up ballet to pursue a career in college teaching. They always seem to think that I quit because I did not like ballet. But they are wrong. I have always liked ballet, and still like it. Perhaps I did not love ballet enough to make the sacrifices (but I made other sacrifices for my Ph.D.). That is only one of the reasons, but not the real reason, for my decision. I gave up ballet because I did not feel completely at ease with body language. I have always expressed myself better with words. Teena made the opposite choice, because she felt that ballet best satisfied her needs for self-expression.

Despite the different careers that we have pursued, we are faced with the same problem in our lecture demonstrations. Both of us have to communicate—I with my words and Teena with her body. We have found that the audience understands both our languages. This experience has made us realize that what really matters is communicating with the means best suited to our personal preferences. And that is why some people choose ballet.

il centro d'incontro per stranieri
palazzo strozzi ammezzato / firenze / telefono 28.39.41

manifestazioni
del mese di
marzo 1977

il centro d'incontro per stranieri è aperto tutti i giorni - domeniche escluse - dalle ore 16 alle 19

giovedì **3** marzo   ore 17

"il balletto
linguaggio del corpo"

presentazione di
joan mammarella m^c connell

dimostrazione di
teena m^c connell

ballerina solista del new york city ballett

Appendix A

Exercises on Barre

Exercises always start to the right, and then are repeated to the left.

1. PLIÉ EXERCISE (MUSIC: 4/4 OR WALTZ)

   2 demi-pliés and 1 grand plié in first position
   repeat in second, fourth and fifth positions
   change from one position to the next with a battement tendu
   hold free arm in second position for demi-plié, and do
       port de bras for the grand plié

2. BATTEMENT TENDU (MUSIC: 2/4 SLOW)

   battement tendu to fourth front, place working foot down in
       fourth front
   plié in fourth and then point front toe
   return to fifth position with a plié
   keep arm in second
   repeat combination en croix

3. BATTEMENT TENDU (MUSIC: 2/4)

   8 battements tendus without plié to the front
   keep arm in second
   repeat combination en croix

4. BATTEMENT TENDU JETÉ (MUSIC: 2/4 ALLEGRO)

   *This combination is done facing the barre with both hands on
       the barre.*

   16 battements tendus jetés to the side with the right leg to
       first position
   repeat to the left
   16 battements tendus jetés to the side with the right leg to
       fifth position (alternate closing first with the right

foot front and end with right foot back)
repeat to the left

5. BATTEMENT TENDU JETÉ (MUSIC: 2/4 ALLEGRO)

4 battements tendus jetés to the front with the right leg
4 battements tendus jetés to the back with the left leg
8 battements tendus jetés to the side with the right leg (alternate closing first to the front and end to the back)
repeat this exercise to the back
keep arm in second

6. ROND DE JAMBE A TERRE (MUSIC: WALTZ)

Preparation: small développé to the front in plié with accompanying arm movement in first position and then carry leg and arm to the second.
16 ronds de jambe à terre en dehors
16 ronds de jambe à terre en dedans
close in fifth front
keep arm in second
port de bras au corps cambré
repeat 3 times
passé relevé (on demi-pointe or pointe) and balance with arms in high fifth

7. ROND DE JAMBE À TERRE (MUSIC: 2/4)

Same preparation as in exercise 6.

2 ronds de jambe (in 2 counts)
3 ronds de jambe (in 2 counts)

repeat 4 times en dehors and 4 times en dedans
keep arm in second

8. FONDU (MUSIC: 2/4 MODERATO OR 4/4)

plié fondu à terre
plié fondu à la demi-hauteur
plié fondu à la hauteur
plié with leg à la hauteur and then close to fifth as working knee is straightened
keep arm in second for the first two fondus
do demi-port de bras for big fondu
repeat en croix

9. FRAPPÉ (MUSIC: 2/4 MODERATO)

2 slow frappés
3 fast frappés
keep arm in second
repeat en croix first with standing leg à plat and then on
     demi-pointe or on pointe
passé into attitude and balance

10. ROND DE JAMBE EN L'AIR (MUSIC: WALTZ)

Start with leg and arm in second.

4 ronds de jambe en l'air en dehors
passé and move arm into low fifth
développé leg front and move arm to first
demi-rond de jambe to second and move arm to second
repeat to the back with rond de jambe en l'air en dedans
turn around on the barre and repeat the combination to the
     left
then repeat the entire combination again to the right and to
     the left on demi-pointe or on pointe

11. BATTEMENT SUR LE COU-DE-PIED (MUSIC: 2/4 ALLEGRO)

4 slow battements sur le cou-de-pied and 8 fast ones with
     accent front
4 slow battements sur le cou-de-pied and 8 fast ones with
     accent back
repeat entire combination on demi-pointe or on pointe
keep arm in low fifth
end combination in fifth with a plié
single or double pirouette en dehors and end in passé relevé
     with one hand on the barre
balance in passé relevé

12. ADAGIO (MUSIC: ADAGIO OR SLOW WALTZ)

passé and développé to the front, grand rond de jambe en l'air en dehors with
     accompanying arm movement, and close leg in fifth back with arm in low fifth
passé and développé to the back, grand rond de jambe en l'air en dedans with
     accompanying arm movement, and close leg in fifth front with arm in low fifth
passé and développé to the second with arm in second
passé and développé to arabesque
slow arabesque penchée and then relevé and balance in arabesque

13. GRAND BATTEMENT (MUSIC: MARCH)

    4 grands battements to the front
    repeat en croix
    keep arm in second

14. STRETCHES

    jambe à la main
    various floor stretches (*see* Chapter 4)

COMMENTS ON THE BARRE EXERCISES

1. Boys do the same exercises on the barre except some of the stretches (such as jambe à la main), which are generally reserved for the girls.
2. When Teena is warming up for a performance, she uses the above barre exercises with the following changes:

    a. She eliminates exercises 5, 7 and 11.
    b. She eliminates the repeats on demi-pointe or on pointe in exercises 9 and 10.

Appendix B

Exercises off Barre

1. (MUSIC: ADAGIO)

   Start in fifth position with right foot front facing croisé.

   grand plié with accompanying arms
   port de bras to the front and raise arms to high fifth and then
       open both arms to second
   passé and développé to second with accompanying arm movement
   relevé with leg à la hauteur and balance
   close back and repeat to the left

2. (MUSIC: 2/4 MODERATO OR 4/4)

   fondu to effacé front in relevé with left arm up
   fondu écarté in relevé with right arm up
   fondu to first arabesque in relevé
   end in fifth back with a plié
   sous-sus with arms in low fifth
   repeat to other side

3. ADAGIO (MUSIC: ADAGIO)

   développé to the front and do grand rond de jambe en l'air en dehors
       and then turn to third arabesque
   tombé with right leg to fourth back and then slide left leg
       into first arabesque
   tour de promenade and end in first arabesque
   arabesque penchée and return to first arabesque
   relevé and tombé to fourth croisé with left leg front
   double pirouette en dehors and end in fifth with right leg back
   repeat to other side

4. PIROUETTES (MUSIC: WALTZ)

Start with right foot in fifth front.

passé relevé and close with right foot front
double pirouette en dehors and land in fourth with right foot
    back
relevé in fourth position with arms in preparatory position for
    pirouette (i.e., right arm in front of chest and left arm
    to the side)
double pirouette and end with right foot in fifth back
repeat to other side

5. SAUTS (MUSIC: 2/4 ALLEGRO)

4 sautés in first with arms in low fifth
3 sautés in second with arms in low second
close to fifth with right foot front
2 échappés closing first to the back and then to the front—use
    accompanying arm movement
4 changements with arms in low fifth
repeat

6. JETÉ (MUSIC: 2/4 ALLEGRO)

Start with right foot back.

jeté and temps levé
repeat
4 jetés
keep arms in low second
repeat entire combination four times

7. ASSEMBLÉ AND SAUT DE CHAT (MUSIC: WALTZ)

Start with left foot front.

glissade with no change of feet, big assemblé to the right and close right foot front
glissade with no change of feet, big assemblé to the left and close left foot front
3 pas de chat to the right, coupé with right leg back and pas de bourrée
repeat to other side

8. FOUETTÉ (MUSIC: 2/4 ALLEGRO)

Preparation: tendu to second.

bring foot to fourth back, plié in fourth and do double
    pirouette en dehors
then 16 to 32 fouettés

9. CODA FROM SWAN LAKE

Start with right foot front.

entrechat quatre and passé with right leg to fifth back
repeat to left
4 échappés with feet changing (on demi-pointe or pointe)
repeat entire combination four times

10. ENTRECHAT (MUSIC: GALLOP)

3 entrechats quatre and 1 royale
arms in low fifth
repeat four times

COMMENTS ON THE OFF-BARRE EXERCISES FOR THE BOYS

1. Instead of exercise 8, the boys could do tour à la seconde
   starting with a battement tendu to second and a pirouette
   en dehors and then begin the series of tours à la seconde.
2. Instead of exercise 9, the boys could do tours en l'air starting
   with sous-sus as a preparation.
3. Instead of exercise 10, the boys could do sous-sus and then entrechat
   six.

Notes

CHAPTER 1. THE BACKGROUND OF BALLET

1. It is indeed an oversimplification to define medieval civilization as otherworldly and Christian, and Renaissance civilization as worldly and pagan. While many aspects of medieval culture emphasized the superiority of the soul, there was always a ribald current which focused on the body. The Middle Ages had developed, however, a magnificent ability to overlook such discrepancies and to absorb variety into the rigid hierarchical system. For example, the Church condemned dance as a pagan pastime, but waived this ban whenever dance was used to praise God. Despite many attempts, the Catholic Church never succeeded in stamping out dance. There are various examples of how dance played an important part in medieval life—St. Vitus's dance, the *Totentanz* or "death dance," tarantism, and the recurrent outbursts of *danseomania* which swept Europe from the eleventh through the fourteenth centuries and culminated in mass dance migrations during the long years of the Black Death.

2. The eighteenth century marked the establishment of many royal opera houses and theaters, some of which had their own ballet companies. The King's Theater in London was opened in 1705; the Royal Danish Ballet, part of the National Theater of Copenhagen, was founded in 1726. The dates of important European opera houses are as follows: 1732 at Covent Garden, 1737 in Naples, 1748 in Vienna, 1750 in Stuttgart, 1752 in Munich, 1776 in Moscow, 1778 in Milan, 1783 in St. Petersburg.

3. August Bournonville (1805–1879), son of a Danish dancer, went to Paris to study under Vestris, and then joined the Paris Opera. He returned to his native Copenhagen and choreographed over thirty ballets, including his own version of Filippo Taglioni's *La Sylphide* for his pupil Lucile Grahn. Bournonville shaped the style and teaching methods of Danish ballet. Contrary to the Romantic ballet tastes of his day, Bournonville considered the male dancers important, and gave them superb training. Today the Bournonville style is still taught in Denmark, and the Danish male dancers are among the world's greatest.

CHAPTER 2. THE BODY AND THE BASIC BALLET POSITIONS

1. There are two variations of fourth position: fourth ouvert, where the leg is "opened" halfway between fourth and second positions, and fourth croisé, where the thighs "cross" but do not touch.

2. The definition of certain positions and steps varies from school to school.

3. The exact position of the hand and fingers varies from school to school. During exercises on the barre, the Cecchetti school requires the student to bend the two center fingers until they almost touch the palm; the French school requires that the second finger and the thumb touch during the barre exercises. Balanchine tells his dancers to practice his correct hand position as follows: they should hold the thumb and all the fingers except the little finger around a small rubber ball, which is cushioned against the palm of the hand. This exaggerated position with the rubber ball makes it easier for them to curve their fingers on stage, and thereby avoid the strained look of tense fingers.

CHAPTER 3. THE BARRE IS NOT A BAR!

1. The first specific reference to the barre can be found in G. Leopold Adice's treatise on dance, *Théorie de la gymnastique de la danse théâtrale* (1857). He used Blasis's class (outlined in the latter's *Code of Terpsichore*) as a model, and specifically stated that the exercises on the barre should last half an hour.

CHAPTER 5. ON YOUR TOES: FOR GIRLS ONLY!

1. One of Camargo's colleagues had fainted on stage from embarrassment after she had ripped her skirt on part of the scenery. This ballerina was obviously terrified of the audience's reaction to her partial, though involuntary, nudity. Values have changed, but most ballerinas still feel a twinge of embarrassment, along with a surge of anger, if their shoulder straps break.

2. The Danish choreographer August Bournonville used very little pointe work in his ballets. Pirouettes and other difficult steps were always performed on demi-pointe. As late as 1950, the Royal Danish Ballet performed his ballets in their original version, and respected this minimum use of pointe work, characteristic of Bournonville's Romantic ballets.

3. The first performance of *Swan Lake,* in 1877, was a total failure, for various reasons. Tchaikovsky's music was too sophisticated for the semi-amateur conductor and too complex for the dancers; both setting and choreography were mediocre. Tchaikovsky attributed this failure to his score, but died before he had time to revise it. The 1880 and 1882 revivals by Hansen fared no better. Finally, in 1895, Petipa and his brilliant assistant Ivanov redid the ballet, which was an immediate success, with Pierina Legnani as Odette-Odile and the Russian Paul Gerdt as Prince Siegfried.

CHAPTER 6. OFF BARRE: THE BEGINNING OF THE CHALLENGE

1. Today new dance studios are often built with a linoleum floor, which offers definite advantages. In addition to being less tiring on the dancers' legs, a linoleum floor reduces both the risk of slipping and the noise factor. In the New York State Theater at Lincoln Center, the floors of the stage and the practice studios are made of linoleum.

CHAPTER 8. THE ADAGIO: BOY MEETS GIRL

1. The following sampling of ages seems to substantiate the longevity theory for dancers: Noverre died at the age of 82, G. Vestris at 79, A. Vestris at 82, Bournonville at 74, Taglioni at 80, Petipa at 91, Johansson at 86, Cecchetti at 78, Zucchi at 83.

Glossary

adagio Musically, adagio refers to a slow tempo. It also describes the slow, flowing yet controlled exercises. Most commonly it is the slow section of the pas de deux.

air, en l' In the air.

allegro Brisk. The term refers to a lively tempo or quick, lively movements.

arabesque A position in which one leg is raised to the back with the arms and head held in a harmonious position. There are many types of arabesque that vary from school to school.

arrière, en Backward.

assemblé Joining together. A jump in which the dancer straightens one leg while he/she kicks the other to second position or fourth front or back. Both feet should land simultaneously in a demi-plié. There are many variations of assemblé.

attitude A pose invented by Carlo Blasis from Giambologna's statue of Mercury. The dancer raises one leg to the back, bends the knee at a 90-degree angle, but keeps the knee higher than the foot. The types of attitude depend on the position of the body, and vary from school to school.

balançoire, en Like a seesaw. For grands battements en balançoire the body leans backward as the leg is kicked to the front, and forward as the leg is kicked to the back.

ballerina A female dancer. In the ballet hierarchy, ballerina or sometimes prima ballerina refers to the outstanding female dancer who performs the top roles. The Czar presented the title of prima ballerina assoluta to two top dancers, Pierina Legnani and Mathilde Kschessinska.

ballet d'action A story ballet like *Swan Lake*.

ballet blanc White ballet. A ballet in which all the dancers wear long white dresses like those introduced by Marie Taglioni in *La Sylphide* in 1832.

ballon Bounce or elevation in jumps.

ballonné Bouncing like a ball. Ballonné is also a jump in which the dancer starts from a demi-plié, performs a battement in the air and lands in a demi-plié with the working foot in the sur le cou-de-pied position.

barre A wooden or metal bar usually attached to the wall. The barre is used for the warm-up exercises.

battement battu Beaten battement. The working toe beats against the ankle of the standing leg with little taps.

battement fondu The standing leg bends into a plié as the working leg moves to the sur le cou-de pied position; then the working leg is extended in any direction. As the leg is extended, the supporting foot may remain flat on the ground or rise to the demi- or full pointe.

battement frappé From the sur le cou-de-pied position, the leg is briskly extended in any direction. Battement frappé can be done double.

battement, grand High kick in any direction with the leg fully extended and the toe neatly pointed. The supporting foot may be flat or in the demi- or full pointe.

battement tendu The working foot slides from the first or fifth position to an open position as the toe brushes the floor. The battement tendu may be done with or without a plié.

battement tendu jeté A battement tendu in which the toe leaves the floor slightly.

batterie Beats (beaten movements) in jumps. The beats can be divided into two basic categories: the batterie à croisement or beats with crossed feet, and the batterie à choc or beats with impact.

box The hard tip of a toe shoe.

break in In ballet jargon, to prepare the toe shoes for performance so that the boxes are neither too hard nor too soft for dancing.

brisé Broken. A jump in which the dancer kicks out one foot, performs an entrechat quatre in the air and lands in demi-plié.

cabriole Goat leap. A jump in which the dancer beats the fully extended legs in mid-air before landing.

cambré Arched. The body is bent from the waist.

classical ballet A style of ballet developed in Russia by the French-born Marius Petipa. His five- to six-act ballets were divided into pantomime sequences and pure dance sections. Russian ballet became world famous with the classical style.

cloche, en Swinging back and forth like a bell. The term refers to a series of grands battements done to the fourth front, then to the fourth back and so forth.

corps de ballet The dancers who do not appear in solo roles.

côté, de Sideways.

cou-de-pied, sur le The foot of the working leg is wrapped around the ankle and the toe is pointed down toward the back of the ankle.

couronne, en The arms are raised over the head in the shape of a crown.

croisé Crossed. One of the two fundamental positions of the épaulement. The body is placed at an oblique angle, and the legs are crossed.

croix, en Like a cross. This term refers to exercises that are done to the fourth position front, to the second position, to the fourth position back and then to the second position, or vice versa.

danseur Male dancer. The title of premier danseur refers to the leading male dancer.

danseuse en travesti A female dancer disguised as a male. The danseuse en travesti danced the male roles during the Romantic period when prejudice against men dancers reached its peak.

déboulés   Rapidly rotating turns in which the dancer steps quickly from one foot to the other while turning. Also called tours châinés.

dedans, en   Inward.

dehors, en   Outward.

détourné   A simple turn (on two feet) in which the dancer turns backward on pointe or demi-pointe in the direction of the back foot.

développé   Developed. The working leg is extended and held in the air. Développé may be done in any direction.

diagonale, en   On a diagonal.

écart, grand   Split. An acrobatic movement used in stretches and in some ballets.

échappé   Escaped. A jump in which the feet move from an odd numbered position (usually fifth but sometimes first) to an even numbered one (second or fourth to the front or back) and then return to the starting position. The échappé can be done on pointe or demi-pointe.

éffacé   Shaded. One of the two fundamental positions of the épaulement. In the French school the direction is called ouvert.

élancer   To dart. One of the seven kinds of movement in classical ballet.

ensellé   Saddled. In this position the back is hollowed and the hips are thrust forward. Not used in classical ballet.

entrechats   Jumps in which the dancer crosses his/her feet in the air. The entrechats are numbered from three on: entrechat trois, entrechat quatre, entrechat cinq and so forth. In the Russian school, the even numbered entrechats end on both feet, and the odd numbered ones on one foot. In the French school the even numbered entrechats cross first to the back, while the odd numbered ones cross first to the front. Entrechat un and entrechat deux do not exist; they are called respectively sauté and changement.

enveloppé   A simple turn (on two feet) in which the dancer does a rond de jambe à terre en dedans and moves the body in a turn to the right.

épaulé   Shouldered. A term used in the Cecchetti method.

épaulement   Shouldering. The placement of the shoulders to add new lines and finish to the movements. Épaulement, a relatively recent invention, was not used in the old French school.

étendre   To stretch. One of the seven kinds of movement in classical ballet.

étiré   Drawn out. This term refers to poses used in supported work.

extension   The dancer's ability to raise and hold the leg as high as possible while still respecting the correct body placement.

face, de   Forward.

fish   Various lifts in which the male dancer supports the female.

fouetté rond de jambe en tournant   A spectacular turn in which the momentum is gained from the whipping circular motion of the working leg. Fouettés are usually done in a series.

glissade   Glide. An important traveling terre à terre step in which the working foot moves from fifth position in the desired direction. Glissade is a transition step.

glisser   To slide. One of the seven kinds of movement in classical ballet.

hauteur, à la   With the leg extended at "full" height—that is, at waist level or higher.

If the leg is held below waist level, it is said to be à la demi-hauteur.

jambe à la main A "classic" stretch for improving extension. The dancer raises her leg in passé, takes the heel in the free hand and extends the leg to the front as she does a plié. Then she moves her leg to the second as she straightens the knee of the standing leg. Finally she releases the heel without lowering the leg.

jeté Thrown. A jump in which the dancer brushes the ground with the working foot as she jumps to the other foot. There are many variations of the jeté.

jeté, grand A large spectacular jeté in which the dancer leaps over an imaginary "hurdle" and lands in a demi-plié on one foot with the other leg in the air.

leg warmers long stockings (usually of wool) that a dancer slips over his/her tights to keep the leg muscles warm. The leg warmers may cover the entire leg or only part of it.

leotard A tightly fitting body garment.

manège, en In a circle.

muscle controlology A system of exercises developed by Joseph Pilates to enable the body to perform at full capacity.

neoclassical A style of ballet developed by George Balanchine as a reaction against Fokine's reforms. Balanchine found his inspiration in the pure dance sequences in Petipa's classical ballets.

pas de bourrée couru A series of small, quick running steps on demi- or full pointe.

pas de deux Dance for two, usually a male and a female.

passé Passed. A transition step in which the pointed toe passes the knee of the supporting leg as the leg goes from one position to another.

penché Leaning.

pirouette Turn. The momentum for a pirouette is gained from the plié and the complementary arm and head movements. Pirouettes may be single or multiple; they may be performed on demi- or full pointe. There is a great variety of pirouettes.

plat, à With the foot flat on the ground.

plié Bent. A bending of the knee or knees. The turnout must be observed, and the knees should be parallel to the toes. If the plié is small (demi-plié), the heels remain on the floor. If the plié is large (grand plié), the heels are slightly raised.

plier To bend. One of the seven kinds of movement in classical ballet.

pointe Toe.

pointe, demi- Half toe.

pointe, sur la Standing on the toes.

pointe, sur la demi- Standing on half toe.

pointe shoes Toe shoes.

poisson See fish.

porté Lift.

position The five basic positions are performed with both feet on the ground. Two "new" positions (sixth and seventh positions) are rarely used in classical ballet.

position, demi- One of the five basic positions performed with the toe of the free foot touching the ground.

position dérivée One of the five basic positions performed with the free leg extended in the air.

positions for toe Today there are two positions for standing on toe: the classical position, where the weight is on the tips of the toes, and the neoclassical position, where the dancer overarches and actually stands on buckled toes.

poussé Pushed. This term refers to poses used in supported work.

profil, de In profile.

raccourci Bent.

raked stage A stage that is perpendicularly inclined toward the audience.

relevé Raised. In a relevé the foot is raised to the demi- or full pointe. Relevé may be done on one or both feet.

relever To raise. One of the seven kinds of movement in classical ballet.

révérence Curtsey.

revolta A difficult jump reserved for the male dancer. He kicks the right foot to the fourth front as he jumps, passes his bent left leg over the right leg as he executes a half turn in the air and then, facing backward, lands on his left leg with the right leg to the fourth back.

romantic ballet A style of ballet that developed in Europe after 1832 (the première of *La Sylphide* danced by Marie Taglioni). The ballerina became an ethereal sylph who transcended earthly limitations and flew upward to the heavens. Toe dancing was introduced during the Romantic period.

rond de jambe à terre A circular movement in which the pointed toe of the working leg describes a semicircle on the floor. The movement may be done outward (en dehors) or inward (en dedans).

rond de jambe en l'air The working leg is extended to the second and describes a small circle in the air by rotating the lower leg from the knee. The circle may be outward (en dehors) or inward (en dedans). The supporting foot may be flat or on the demi- or full pointe.

royale A changement done with a beat. The royale is often called a changement battu.

saut de chat Cat jump. A jeté in which the dancer pulls up both knees as high as he/she can before landing on both feet in a plié.

sauter To jump. One of the seven kinds of movement in classical ballet.

seconde, à la To the second position.

shank The thick leather inner sole of a toe shoe.

sickle To roll one's weight toward the little or big toe instead of concentrating it on the ball of the foot.

sissonne A jump named after its inventor. Here the dancer leaps into the air, kicks out one leg before landing, and ends in a demi-plié with the working leg extended. There are many variations of the sissonne.

sobresaut A jump in which the dancer straightens both legs directly under him/her, moves forward and lands in a demi-plié.

soloist A position between the corps de ballet and the ballerina or danseur in the dance hierarchy.

sous-sus Under-over. The sous-sus is a relevé in which the dancer springs on demi- or full pointe and travels in any direction with the feet held tightly together.

spotting The movement of the head in turns to minimize dizziness. The dancer chooses a fixed point in the distance and "spots" on it as he/she turns.

temps simples   Simple movements.

terre à terre   On the ground. This term refers to steps in which the feet never leave the ground at the same time.

tights   Various colored nylon "pantyhose."

tour à l'Italienne   A tour relevé in second position. This tour is a male specialty.

tourner   To turn. One of the seven kinds of movement in classical ballet.

tour piqué   A turn in which the dancer steps on one foot (on demi- or full pointe) and turns, usually with the leg in passé. The turns may be single or multiple. Tours piqués may be done with the working leg in attitude or in arabesque.

tour sauté   Aerial turn.

tours chaînés   *See* déboulés.

turnout   The dancer's ability to turn legs and feet at a 180-degree position from the hips. The turnout is a fundamental principle of classical ballet.

tutu   A classical costume with a short skirt made of many layers of net. The Romantic tutu reaches midcalf.

vamp   The front part of the box of a toe shoe.

variation   A solo dance.

volé   Flying.

Index